The Art of Seduction

The Art Of Approach And The Psychology Of Attraction - A Guide To Becoming The Ideal Partner For Every Woman

(The Key To Captivating A Woman's Heart: Achieving Mastery In The Art Of Attraction, Establishing Genuine Connections, And Utilizing Emotional Triggers For Potent Seduction)

Walter Cheung

TABLE OF CONTENT

Screening Method 1

Arrogance is NOT cool; confidence is 11

L'ART OF SEDUCTIVE FRAGRANCE: L'AROMATIQUE 34

The added value 60

A BETTER PARTNER FOR HIS OR HER PLEASURE 85

A Seduction Win 97

Screening Method

One person will always be the pursuer and the other the pursued in any courtship. Therefore, when you are pursued, you are at the mercy of the pursuit, which screens the pursuer. This usually occurs when you approach a female in an attempt to win her over. Your goal is to leave a positive impression. Perhaps you're buying her drinks, perhaps you're complimenting her. Perhaps you're attempting to be as amusing as possible, like a dancing monkey. Since you've previously shown her all of your cards, you may be simply paying her a lot of attention, and she is deciding when to get serious.

Clearly, you're willing to put in more effort than she is, and the one who exerts more effort to maintain the interaction—the one who is more invested in the conversation continuing—has less social influence. And that's the individual undergoing screening. But when you turned this around, you made the female come out of her screening mode. Most girls begin to screen guys as soon as they meet them. And one of the first things they look for is whether or not they find that individual attractive. Does he behave normally, or is he acting strangely, jittery, and nervous? Subsequently, people begin to question, "Am I attracted?" Then they begin to wonder, are we a good fit? Would He be someone with whom my friend would go out? How would my life be structured? They ask, "What would I feel like if I were dating this guy? Or if I were hanging out with him?" etc. That's the screening frame, and it's not very useful to us because a lady is searching for reasons not to like you within the screening period. She searches for errors in things. We want to turn this around because, when you do the opposite and begin screening her first, you drive the girl to go from screening herself to justifying and qualifying herself and pursuing you in an attempt to gain your favor. That results from passing the screening process. You feel great when you seek a girl, and she chooses you since you worked hard for her. Later on, we'll also discuss the psychological theory of investment that plays a role in this.

For now, though, all we need to know is to turn the tables and encourage the female to pursue rather than just put her in screening mode and have her justify and qualify herself! This is a little trickier to start with. Many men struggle with the practical application of many of these ideas because they wonder when to get started. When it comes to enticing girls to chase you, it's very easy. You have to be somewhat attractive to a female before you try to persuade her to pursue you; this means that she has to be open to moving with you or proving herself. You shouldn't start chasing her if she hasn't been willing to move somewhere with you and if she won't even qualify for the relationship. This is a crucial matter.

She's just not that interested; therefore, you don't want to start attempting to utilize any of these strategies. When we talk about compliance and momentum, you'll see that if you try to encourage a female to chase you and she refuses, you'll have a harder time pursuing her throughout the encounter because the more times you ask her no, the more probable it is that she will say no. You've isolated her as soon as you start to feel some attraction. She's one-on-one if she's with a group or if you've moved her around a bit. You want to use qualification and disqualification to entice girls to chase you, even if it's just a few feet away. And we're going to start by discussing that. Therefore, qualifying is the first step in getting a female to chase you. First of all, qualifying establishes the parameters within which you are genuinely screening her.

I'm showing a girl that I'm not just interested in any lady if I say, "You seem like a typical party girl." I'm letting her know that I'm not quite sold on her yet and that she still has work to do before I can fully commit to her. So, even though I could find her physically attractive, I won't approve of her until she proves otherwise. She won't simply win my approval by talking to me and being attractive. Many guys find that when they initiate conversation with girls, they immediately become incredibly thrilled that the girls are interested in them. You know, they never consider moving forward. They don't consider offering the girl reasons why they like her, nor do they consider having the girl struggle to earn your favour and prove her worth.

Recognize the Desires of Women

As the book's title suggests, one of the keys to dating successfully is discerning and comprehending what your partner wants.

While it can be a little complex, this is not as hard as most people think. All you need to do is ascertain what your significant other desires from you. Most women are not interested in informing you; instead, you should observe her every action and read her body language and facial emotions.

There is nothing in this world as convoluted as a woman's feelings. Women often experience mood swings, which can be attributed to a variety of physiological changes and psychological effects. She will go from being joyful and confident to sobbing like a toddler in an instant, even though you may not be aware of this.

It's not just you; the majority of men experience this issue. So, don't worry about that. This is not inherently wrong in itself; they are simply being ladies. This allows you to express your concern and your willingness to listen to her whenever she needs to hear it. It can be difficult to anticipate and comprehend how someone else is feeling or what she expects from you when you first start dating, but trust me when I say that if you accept and embrace her for who she is and make an effort to not only understand her but also make accommodations for her, she will adore you.

Many men in committed relationships with women are occasionally surprised when their girlfriends exhibit such irregular or unpredictable outbursts. But they don't realize that's when their manliness is tested, and they have to prove they are the men they say they are. Things could quickly go south when a guy reacts poorly in these situations.

Consequently, the mystery of what a woman desires has long been a subject of discussion and in-depth study. How, then, is it possible for a simple guy like you to know that? I'm here to help. Based on in-depth research, expert trials, and my experience from interacting with people of the opposite sex, I've put together some incredible insights that will help you grasp what your girlfriend wants from you.

Little things count.

Though it's common knowledge that women are incomprehensible and difficult to understand, give her some more time to be explored. Women may seem complex and distinct from one another at first glance. However, they have certain fundamental needs and demands that they expect their partner to meet on a deep level. No matter how tough or reckless they seem on the outside, everyone is emotional at heart and needs someone to look out for them. However, it's also important for you as a guy to respect them and understand that they cannot take care of themselves even though they want you by their side. They desire an abundance of love and care from you. They will always be there to support and appreciate you, no matter what you are going through, and they will be there for you no matter what.

It is a common misconception among males that women always desire expensive and flashy gifts, but this isn't always true. All that women desire is your attention and your ears. It's possible that your lady has been chatting about a specific café where she had amazing pastries and simply adored it, or she may have mentioned how much she desired a new kitchen appliance she had seen at a friend's house and how helpful it was. You can see that even though she is more than capable of obtaining those items, she wants you to purchase them for her if you listen to their conversations with little attention. Purchase a box of those pastries the next time you see her, or give her the appliance for your upcoming big day. She will love you more for this.

Your SHE desires E

Remind yourself that the letter E, in this instance, stands for the word EFFORT. Your significant other expects you to make a greater effort to support her or work on your relationship. You might be wondering how any female could truly appreciate you for taking the time to make this tiny but significant effort. Occasionally, without being asked, surprise her by cleaning the dishes or bringing out the garbage.

Make a lovely meal for your lady love when she gets home from work, and you can spend some quality time with her instead of bringing her out to a fancy restaurant, even though it sounds tempting. In order to give her some downtime and relaxation, you might also plan a surprise spa day for her for the weekend. She will put more effort into you and your relationship in exchange.

Arrogance is NOT cool; confidence is

Like everyone else, girls are drawn to self-assured men. You must exude confidence in everything you do, including how you approach her. Girls adore spending time with someone who exudes certainty, security, and confidence. You will be able to make choices since you are a self-assured man. Girls want you to be confident in your desires and intelligent. For them, confidence is just as crucial as intelligence regarding what makes men appeal to women.

But even if women value confidence much, don't overdo it if it could become conceited. You should always remember that a very narrow line separates confidence from arrogance. Although all women aspire to be self-assured men, they dislike haughty men. Being conceited will prevent you from leaving a positive, long-lasting impression on her; on the contrary, it will drive her away from you.

We value chivalry. Yes, you may believe that today's girls are self-assured and strong-willed. They are capable of caring for themselves. However, the truth is that every lady secretly enjoys being spoilt and indulged by her spouse. Even though she presents you with an image of strength and maturity, she still harbours a childlike belief in fairies. Indeed, she is still waiting for her ideal partner to show up. It doesn't require you to ride a horse or engage in any similar activity. But sure, you can communicate your politeness and humble attitude to her by particular gestures. She will love you even more if you pay for your first date and hold the door for her. Thus, the next time, try some timeless dance movements and watch how amazed your partner gets.

Be not a baby.

Women are indeed predisposed to looking after and nurturing their cherished ones. But it doesn't imply that you start treating her like your mother and expect her to nurture you. No woman desires to be your mother. You'll believe that showing compassion is among the most essential things your lady enjoys doing for you. However, the reason she looks after you is because she loves you. This does not imply, however, that you rely too heavily on her. Though every man is a child at heart, women want to be taken care of by you; they do not want to be your mother or caregiver. Therefore, remember that and try not to act like a child in front of your partner; if you do, she will end the relationship.

The best policy is to be honest.

Never, ever tell a lie to a woman. They can sense when you are hiding something from them; therefore, even if you believe you can trick her, she can figure it out because they have a sixth sense. She may appear persuaded by your explanations, but underneath, she may begin to look into the matter more. The cornerstones of any partnership ought to be honesty and open communication.

A false and dishonest foundation will not allow a relationship to last long. For this reason, never lie to your girlfriend under any circumstances. If she discovers that she has been misled, her damaged trust will take some time, if it ever heals at all, to mend despite several justifications and expressions of regret. Therefore, don't let a falsehood jeopardize your important relationship. Conversing with your partner and informing her of any discrepancies in your perspectives and opinions is preferable. Tell her you appreciate her but also have other things that require your attention. Don't be unfaithful to your girlfriend; a man who can't maintain faithfulness in a relationship isn't worthy of one.

Section 1

The rain came down hard on me as I rushed through the streets. I could not find cover as it seeped into my eyes and soaked my clothes. I would miss the last train and be stranded for the night if I didn't get to the station in time. I had to leave this area immediately and head home to my bed.

Numerous individuals ran alongside me, sharing my identical objective, yet their actions only impeded my progress. They were too erratic and too slow. They obstructed me and confined me, causing my body to twitch with annoyance. I attempted to force my way through them, but they proved to be an impenetrable wall.

I slammed into the back of the girl in front of me, who had paused to check her phone.

"Be careful," I shouted, shoving her away.

I had no chance of making it. Such elegant shoes. It would have been easy to run if I had worn sneakers, but these high heels made it difficult. My feet slid about because the wetness had seeped into them. I was completely unmotivated. The last straw would be if I tripped and twisted my blasted ankle. But I had to keep going.

As I ran, the rain made puddles in the street and splashed my legs. The neon lights glistened on the damp surfaces all around me.

Tokyo was something I detested.

Since my arrival a month ago, I have detested it daily.

They'd said, do a student exchange. It will improve your resume. They had said to do a homestay. We are a wealthy and aristocratic family. They are renting out their opulent property for homestays. Although it sounded like a dream, it was a nightmare. I made a lot of mistakes. My mental compass, which distinguished between good and bad, intelligent and foolish, and decent guy and jerky dickwad, appeared to have completely flipped.

I hadn't even desired to visit Japan or Tokyo. All I had wanted was to get out, and this swap had seemed like the ideal way to do it. At the last minute, the school had covered all costs, including a special scholarship for underprivileged children. I was that person—poor and itching to get away.

At the lights, the crowd of people came to a halt. The most famous junction in the world was even more congested than normal as all the office workers and drinkers raced for their trains. The only individuals hanging around were those with nowhere better to go or children heading to clubs.

All I had to do was cross the road and enter the station. I could pull it off. I could dash up the stairs to my train and go through the ticket barrier first if I beat everyone else. It was Platform 8 that I required. Keeping an eye on the goal.

I shuffled to the front, avoiding any umbrella within eyeshot distance of me while we waited. I loomed over them in my shoes, already much taller than most girls here. That only increased the risk associated with the umbrellas.

I reached the front, my shoe tip brushing the curb. I exhaled and ran away as soon as the lights came on. If it meant my death, I would take that train.

I'd make it. Of course, I would make it.

However, the lights went out right as I arrived. I nearly let out a cry as I glanced up at the monitors. I'd missed the train. At 5.38 am was the following one. More than four hours had elapsed. Four hellish hours.

I just gazed as if the facts would magically shift. A staff member arrived and lowered the entrance doors. Without a doubt, the station was closed.

I felt like kicking that door. All I wanted to do was board a train and return home safely, even if the city was bustling around me.

After I stopped jogging, I started to feel cold. I had a jacket, but I had given it to doucheface Kenji in the hotel room. I would never go back and retrieve it. The hypothermia would kill me first. I vowed never to see that jizz rag once more.

I was unable to move. Stuck. I needed to kill time and warm up. I would much rather murder that jerk, Kenji. He'd gotten me into this situation. Our once-passionate evening had turned into a horrible night. Still, a ray of hope came through me. It's far better to be stuck outside the station in the rain than alone with him.

I sat on a bench because I could not get much wetter. Individuals were circulating outside the station. A few of them were inebriated. A few were inebriated and passed out. A few unscrupulous characters and several couples. Now, there was a little drizzle, distorting the billboard lights.

I got some strange looks because of the damp t-shirt sticking to my body. Usually, after seeing my tattoos, folks quickly moved away. God, a pair of tats wouldn't even be given a second thought. Here, I felt like a murderer with an axe. However, that wasn't sufficient to ward off the creepers on a late night outside the station. It appeared to draw them in.

My makeup must have run down my face in black lines as my hair stuck to my face.

Among the men hanging around, at least three of them sneered at my tits. To hide myself, I pulled at the collar of my shirt. I regretted dressing seductively on several occasions.

I thought it would be enjoyable when I got dressed for the evening. Kenji and I had gone out with some other classmates occasionally. He then asked me to have a drink by myself. We had begun discussing love hotels. I couldn't help but be fascinated.

"That's possible," he stated.

"A hotel of love?"

I wanted to know what it was about, even if I wasn't into him. Kenji wasn't really attractive. Though I wasn't terribly in love with him or anything, he didn't make me uncomfortable either.

He hadn't turned me off till now, though.

Why had I even accepted to accompany him to a love hotel? If I probed the dark recesses of my being, I would have to concede that my hunger for his cock was secondary to my loneliness. He hadn't treated me like an oddball among the few guys I'd met. He seemed to genuinely enjoy me when he spoke with me.

I had been incredibly mistaken.

I had made it clear that I didn't want him to touch my neck in any way. I detest getting touched there. Before we entered that foolish hotel room, he seemed okay with following my instructions.

Then he had carried it out. There, he had touched me.

I'd jumped away from him and yelled.

"I warned you against doing that."

He scowled me.

"Stop being so rigid. It was quite slight. I assumed foreign girls were willing to try anything. particularly ones like you," he remarked sarcastically.

With my backpack in hand, I bolted out of the room.

Asking wasn't unreasonable. Why was he not able to hear me out?

That's because girls like me. Guys were not as receptive to girls like myself. They simply grabbed what they desired.

The materials I had brought were still unused in the bottom of my backpack. I read them through. A change of clothes would be nice, provided I could locate a place to change.

Condoms — they were a pointless waste of money. I pondered whether a nearby couple would be interested in purchasing them from me.

Snack foods – score. I had neglected to include them in my backpack.

I removed a chocolate with my fishing net. I tore the wrapper off and gave it a taste. Oh, chocolate, my devoted companion. Eating it even made me feel warmer. The sweet delight made me feel content and provided me with energy. For a little moment, the awful reality vanished. The exquisite chocolate and I were all that was present.

Section

YOU

To begin with, let me tell you there is nothing wrong with you. Perhaps it's the words you choose, the faces you make (no one likes a scary face), or even your hairstyle, but nothing about who you are today is incorrect; nothing matters more than loving yourself. It is impossible to give away what you do not have, and it is also impossible to force others to experience emotions that you do not yourself. How can you expect someone else to love you if you don't love yourself? Someone who might not even be aware of your existence at this moment.

Although it seems obvious now, no one had previously informed me of this. I was annoying myself because I didn't have the ideal hairstyle, nose, or haircut. I was angry that I wasn't more attractive and worried about my height. Put another way, I expected people to love and care for me even if I hated myself.

Basic self-love is accepting yourself for who you are; your height, skin tone, nose, eyebrows, hands, feet, hair colour, and skin tone are all wonderful features that make you unique. Occasionally, hug and kiss in the mirror when you wake up, tell yourself that you are beautiful every morning, love yourself more than anything else, and embrace every part of your body. Love for oneself attracts love for others; when you are confident in yourself, you radiate that confidence to others and encourage others to feel the same way about you. It resembles an artist who pours his soul into each brushstroke while painting a landscape. It's not the painting's technique that will cause it to sell for a million dollars; rather, the artist's love and passion for his medium will give the piece its $1 million value. All three artists—Van Gogh, Picasso, and Leonardo da Vinci—shared a deep love and enthusiasm for their work, which they instilled in the viewers of their paintings, inspiring them to feel the same way.

The secret to sex appeal is loving yourself, but use caution because this is a two-edged sword: excessive or illogical love can also lead to careless appearance choices. I'll give you an example to help you understand. A man opened a restaurant with just five dishes and a small staff. The food was good enough to eat again, but it wasn't a five-star establishment; it was somewhere you could go once a week to enjoy some good food and beer with friends. The proprietor devoted all his time to the restaurant, essentially making it his home, leaving little time for other pursuits. The restaurant's owner cleaned the tables and the establishment at night so that it would look nice the next day so he could sleep all morning till opening. The restaurant opened at 11:00 am and closed at 11:00 pm every day. The owner truly had a fantastic space; it was bright and comfortable and had everything a restaurant needs—except one crucial element: patrons.

The owner soon became concerned as he had made significant investments and was not receiving any returns. He had to spend a lot of time inside keeping the kitchen tidy, the tables set, and the floors swept. He worked so hard inside the restaurant that he seldom ever left. Everything in his life revolved around the restaurant. The most evident thing occurred at the end: he had to close, all of the time, money, and effort invested was gone, and the bills kept coming in. The owner fell into deep despair and seldom left the house until he was finally forced to leave. Stepping outside, he looked at the front of the restaurant, where he saw people distributing drugs, an old dumpster with an awful stench, graffiti on the walls, a homeless man living next to the dumpster, and a cracked, damp sidewalk from a broken pipe. The owner realized what was wrong at that moment; he had been focusing too much on the interior and neglected to glance outside. He had the best location but didn't let patrons go near enough to see it.

Accept and respect who you are, and invest in your self-worth without sacrificing your appearance. Even the most pricey diamond requires polishing. To ensure that your look is not a barrier, we need to cover a few basic things. Don't worry; you won't require aesthetic surgery, but you may have to pay some money. We will address it in a later section of this chapter.

Men and women think and are drawn to different things. For example, men may find women attractive or overweight, tall or short, have dark or light hair, have no hair at all or in the Chewbacca style, have light or brown eyes, have a full beard or none at all. Many things can make you appear hotter or less, or things that you may believe will make you appear more beautiful to someone but have the opposite effect. At this point, you ask, "How would I know what I must do or look like to be liked?" The solution is straightforward: start by considering what women DON'T like in a man and act accordingly, rather than considering what they like in a man. Consider the most absurd and apparent ideas. Would you date a person with onion breath if you were a girl?

Since everyone seems to know the solution, you already know what she would never like, so go in the other direction. Purchase mouthwash, antibacterial toothpaste, and a new toothbrush at the drugstore. Frequently, we concentrate on the qualities we believe girls enjoy and ignore what they find objectionable. As a result, we neglect to groom in favour of attempting to appear fitter, taller, or even tanner.

Let's start with terrible breath. Even if you don't think you have it, you may, as it's something that occasionally, even your closest friends may withhold from you out of concern that you'll look foolish. Almost no one will tell you to your face if they give you a sing-along or offer you a piece of gum. Therefore, I strongly advise you to go buy that toothbrush, toothpaste, and mouthwash.

Not related to food. If you recently had tacos, you will smell like onions, but this should only last a few hours. If the smell persists, you should pay closer attention to what you're putting in your mouth. You should be able to notice an improvement in both your breath and the appearance of your teeth, which are gradually becoming whiter and cleaner.

If your issue is more serious, cleaning your teeth won't always solve it since, similar to taco breath, it will initially smell minty after brushing, but it will fade after a few hours, returning your breath to its normal unpleasant flavour.

Chamomile Tea. This is one of the greatest ways to get rid of bad breath. There are a lot of different home remedies and methods you may try, such as rinsing your mouth with baking soda and salt, but I promise you don't want to taste that way every day. God be praised for the chamomile! The tea made from this flower is so beneficial that people also use it as an anti-inflammatory, analgesic, and digestive tonic to promote healthy skin and hair and to alleviate anxiety. However, the property that interests us the most is its "Antibacterial" properties. Recall that bacteria is the source of bad breath. Here's the cure: have a cup of chamomile tea in the morning and use another cup as a mouthwash before bed. This is quite effective; in addition to improving your breath, you also benefit from all the other qualities this tea contains.

When pursuing a female, this is something we tend to overlook, but it's also one of the first things you should be concerned about: how can you expect to win her over if she can't even talk to you without feeling sick to her stomach? And forget about kissing her.

Problem solved! From now on, when we chat with her, our breath won't get in the way, and she won't say, "Oh my god, your breath smells great!" But trust me, even though it's something she instinctively expects from a male, she will remember.

Now, considering we are attempting to be quite clear, let's consider another thing a girl wouldn't enjoy. Would a female find someone wearing "un-fashionable" clothing attractive? You should be aware by now that the response is, "Oh, hell no! This is significant, especially for women who are not interested in fashion. Unless you both run for the same team, women have the best sense of style when it comes to fashion. Therefore, invest in casual footwear instead of tennis shoes and dress for success.

L'ART OF SEDUCTIVE FRAGRANCE: L'AROMATIQUE

I used to go shopping at the mall with my pals every Friday night when I was fifteen. We regularly visited a bath and body shop to slather ourselves in fruit-flavoured body lotion. I used to sneak into the store's back area, where the priciest items were showcased, and fill up my cart when nobody else was around. Load up, in this context, refers to taking out a piece of index card from my wallet and misting it with Woodland cologne. I was utterly enamoured with my crush but was too scared to pursue our relationship. It was the scent that he wore. Keeping him in my wallet was a lot simpler. If that boy could only see me now! hehe

Let's investigate the art of alluring scent, a potent and enchanted craft. Let's start with a little physics lecture explaining why scent is important to sensuality and seduction. A bundle of nerves in the nose known as the olfactory system receives scents when we breathe them in. The limbic system—the area of the brain and mind that controls memory and emotion—is strongly tied to this system. Therefore, I could make my heart race and my thighs quiver simply by keeping that small card in my wallet, bringing it out, and inhaling deeply!

Still, there's more to alluring scent than just dousing oneself in gardenia and hoping for the best. Indeed, going overboard might have the exact opposite impact. Sciolino speaks with renowned French perfumer Jean-Claude Ellena in the book. (He held out his arm as if to push her away.) Perfume works almost like a shield.

This Seductive Fragrance Anointing Ritual will help you link the power of your intention with the power of your fragrance. While I adore my perfumes, I prefer essential oils for this ritual because they are extremely potent and aromatherapeutic. Because they come from natural sources, you run a much lower risk of offending or off-putting someone when applying them in the quantity needed for this ritual. Essential oils are like the blood of plants.

When you walk down the street after you have completed this process, people will be staring at you and wanting to approach you closer, and they will be confused about why they can't bear to be apart from you.

Waiting for Laura to come back is wearing on my nerves. Is this all there is to it? Will Laura just disappear without a word?

Her public accusation angered me, but it subsided when I saw her tiredness, the sadness in her eyes, and her white knuckles. It was obvious that coming here cost her, but whatever the rights and wrongs of it, she genuinely believed in the mission she assigned herself tonight. She's not an actress; her face conveys her emotions as clearly as a picture book. Now that she's gone, I'm edgy and bored. Suddenly, the only person at this damn party I want to talk to is her.

She's always been great at fielding phone calls from ex-flames, too. She's probably protected me from all sorts of things over the years. I don't do paperwork. One of the great things about success is the ability to delegate all the boring stuff in life to other people. All in all, her story seems true. Marie might have tossed the letters in the bin had they not been formalized by a lawyer's letter.

The annoying platinum blonde who keeps grabbing my arm and leans forward to show me her surgically enhanced cleavage is cooing in a foolish young girl's voice.

Same old, same old, but tonight, it grates on my nerves. I want to find Laura. She looked beautiful in the soft light cast by the terrace up-lighters. If she looks that good in a black skirt and white blouse, I can only imagine how she'd look with a chiffon gown skimming her beautiful curves, her auburn waves swept up into a top knot. Or even better, wearing nothing at all, her hair loose, trailing over her bare breasts...

Inspiration has struck at a perfect moment, and it has selected a woman who despises me and all I stand for. Wonderful. I know this silent surge of creative obsession will grow more persistent if I try to ignore it.

I can't wait to paint her, so I'm already figuring out how to perfectly capture her essence and personality on canvas. My fingers are itching for charcoal and a sketchpad so I can start doing preliminary sketches.

I gently pull my arm away from the sly blonde, but she has a vice-like grip on me, and her breath smells like booze.

She sneers, "Hey, where are you going, Jack? We barely got started."

"And we never will," she says, clinging to me and lurching against me as her red wine spills over my shirt as I reluctantly pull harder to break free of her grasp.

Amazing

Eventually, I freed myself and pried her fingers from my arm, my annoyance growing. I have to change now, so I won't wait for Laura's return if Laura hurryes.

I think I must be dreaming that somehow I have II'veconjured Laura fast while sleeping on my bed, but before I even enter the bedroom door, I have already unbuttoned my shirt. I close the door behind me, my sixth sense warning me not to disturb her.

She looks so striking, her red hair fanned out around her unfashionably pale complexion. There is no fake bake here; I'm relieved to see. As an artist, I object to this trend of painting every human the same pigment - TOWIE orange. I don't understand why looking like you've been Tangoed is considered a sexy look.

I can't even breathe for fear of waking her. Still, instead of the bed or the monochrome outfit, I picture WWaterhouse'sOphelia, innocently beguiling and breathtakingly beautiful, resting in a June meadow.

I can't stand to break the enchantment that turns my bed into a canvas, so I swallow hard. Her lips are slightly parted, only showing her tiny pink tongue. Should I wake her?

I pull out my bedside drawer and quietly grab the sketchpad and piece of charcoal I keep in case inspiration strikes, and I start drawing.

Laura stirs, but I'm still working.

She mumbles, "Sophie, is that you? Would you believe I've II'vefallen asleep in my clothes again? Oh," as she gets up onto her elbows.

She glances at me, my notepad, and my bare chest, blinking quickly and staring at me with an endearingly blurry uncertainty that defies explanation. Eventually, she gives a little shake of her head and looks up.

A look of fear crossed her features, and I fought the impulse to chuckle. "Er, I'm sorry, I fell asleep. I was just making a call, not waiting for you."""" h?" I ask, completing my drawing as if this were a normal scenario." did you eat my porridge before you tried out my bed? Though I'd say, you're more of a Sleeping Beauty than a Goldilocks. Or maybe a Red Riding Hood? I wondered if I had to kiss you to wake you up." That could have been entertaining, hmm. It's too bad she woke up before I had this idea.

"What are you doing? If II'mRed Riding Hood, does that make you the wolf?" she asks, fixing her gaze on my sketchpad.

Some people call it art, but it's just me making stuff up and trying to make the world see things my way.

"ll right," Laura says, looking tired and lost as she clambers. I extend my arm to assist her, but she only scowls and turns away.

She looks down at the floor and says," "here... something I have to say. You know you really shouldn't have moved," "I say, scowling as I turn to face my pad again. ""mm?"" I ask, sensing something is off. I detest this feeling.

With all the care she's sending them, it seems more like she's apologizing to her shoes than to me. "Hat? Look, I wanted to say I'm sorry, really sorry. You...might have been right.""""ay, have been, "I ask, wrinkling my eyebrows.

After setting down my notebook, I approach Laura until I can smell her scent—floral but not like any perfume I've ever worn—and I wonder if it will cling to my sheets.

1. During an IKEA purchase

We all know that IKEA is the most confusing place ever and that following a bunch of arrows through a massive blue warehouse to save £3.50 on a table lamp isn't even close to sexy. Still, if you follow these pointers, you can ensure that the Billy bookcase is the only thing you bring into your bedroom tonight.

Start by drawing attention to yourself in the bedroom. Lie sensually, modelling possible stances for later. If that doesn't work, try leaping out of a closet. The element of surprise never goes underappreciated!

Follow your target throughout IKEA and give them helpful advice while they're there. For example, if they're looking at carpets, mention that you might have a shag pile with their name on it.

If none of this gets the desired response, use the kitchen department's offers to hone your seduction skills. Turkey basters, rolling pins, and piping bags all have erotic overtones that will make it more likely that you'll hit it lucky before you get to the flat-packed furniture.

Another extreme tactic is to steal your sultry customer cart so you can step in and pretend to be someone who can assist them in finding it. This should make it more likely that they will follow you around the store, allowing you to guide them into a less frequented but isolated area of the establishment—the restroom area. Create a lot of noise about how big the tubs are, then jump into one, declaring that you are stuck and need assistance being pulled out by tugging on your rear.

Once your persistent haranguing has paid off, you'll have won over your fellow customers. Invite them to enjoy some traditional Swedish food in the cafe to seal the deal. The meatballs will remind them of the night's pleasures, and at just 90p for a refillable soft drink, it's an excellent value for budget-conscious diners.

If all goes well, you should be headed back home with your conquest in half the time it would take to assemble one of IIKEA's bedside tables. All you need to do now is make your journey home, this time with more than just some tinned herring to be excited about upon your return.

Right now, the only thing on your mind is the precise location of the act. Just be sure it's not on an IKEA bed, as there's a 96% chance it will collapse.

2. As I was seeing some Van Gough paintings at the London National Gallery

These days, art has lost much respect compared to hundreds of years ago. These days, to sell your work, you have to sell yourself, possibly through the medium of both performance art and shock value, such as two girls shitting into a cup and eating it (Google it) or an installation piece that is the unmade bed that you spent several days shitting in, pissing in and producing any other bodily fluids you can muster, all symbolically intertwined to convey the elusive message of world hunger.

If you're not inspired by modern art, you might be better off going to the National Gallery, where you'll find several art hippies soaking in each other's quiet seclusion. You could also have the opportunity to practice some free-hand techniques with another seductive artist there.

As annoying as it may be, you just need to keep in mind that many working artists have their heads stuck in their butts because of conflicts between their ego and their failure to have a real profession. After all, you only need to steer clear of those who paint themselves.

Since sadness and suicide are more likely to come up in conversation with an aspiring artist who may be reclusive and withdrawn than romance and sex, this is a great starting place.

Van GGogh's major themes in his work are probably depression and suicide.

Talk about how many self-portraits Van Gogh painted, then present a few of your own—they could just be regular phone selfies you Photoshop-edited to look like paintings since many artists are easily fooled by technology and drawn to your original illusion.

Recall that the more provocative, insane, and macabre the art, the more interest it will arouse. Therefore, play a voyeuristic video of your parents having sex, then your pets having sex, and finally, you having sex with yourself. Let your target complete their interpretation of what they have just seen and accept it all the same; the video should also allude to the main theme you are working on. This will validate their distinct perspective and give your confident artist the much-needed boost in confidence. It will also make you appear even more sophisticated and sophisticated.

Since all artists must paint naked to avoid staining their overalls, an aartist'sstudio is the most romantic place for unleashing contained passion; hopefully, this time, however, you will be chaotically throwing hard, wet strokes at something other than your canvas to make a masterpiece representing sexual gratification. With your suitor's attention firmly fixed on you and your amazing art, now direct their attention on returning to your basement to see a work-in-progress nude self-portrait in your "studio."

Section 4

I had to make him wait a minute because I didn't want him to believe I was overly excited about our date. Ring, Ring, Ring... I answered on the third, realizing it was Money.

II'moutdoors, sexy. Hey.

""See, now. Give me a moment."""" o you require me to rise?"""" o, head straight down." I was a little uneasy after I hung up and wondered why I felt that way.

I ran to the elevator and hurried to his car, and Money opened the door for me again like a gentleman. However, when I went to sit, I noticed a big shopping bag on the seat. I could tell it was a Victoria's Secret bag from a distance, so I managed to peek inside and saw lingerie. I lifted the bag and put it on my lap. Money closed my door and skipped over to his. Before I could thank you, he reached behind my seat and got something, his chest all in my face. I smelled the fresh scent of his cologne, which was so delightful. I closed my eyes and let the scent take over me; the noise of plastic crumbling made me horny. I heard a plastic crumbling noise, so I opened my eyes and saw Money holding a bouquet.

"I remember the last time I had a bouquet, but thanks, they are tthey'rebeautiful," I lied.

Money questionedSeriouslysly?" I said, "Seriously.""""If I were your husband, I would send you flowers daily. That muthafucka doesn't know the beautiful flower that he has," Money said, grasping the wheel.

Money moved into a relaxed position and placed his right hand on my thigh. I didn't move or give him any indication that I didn't want him to touch me. I relaxed and enjoyed the music as he drove us back to the downtown area. I didn't object to or agree with his statement, and I didn't want to open any doors that didn't need to be opened.

I was at a loss for words as Money parked the car next to a Bentley coupe and looked at me, waiting for me to say something. I had no idea where he was taking me, and this building looked even more run-down than the chicken shack he had taken me to. The building looked like an abandoned manufacturing building that had been out of business for decades. We pulled up in front of a brick-red building covered in graffiti. A tall black fence surrounded the building.

"It'scool. Trust me." Money grinned.

I asked, giving him a weird look," are you sure?" He smiled and said," "es, it gets better inside.""" Right, if you say so.""""" That's awesome.""" "Remember to bring your bag," "Money said, pointing to the underwear bag as he came around the car to open my door. He laughed as I danced on the rocks toward the door and helped me walk on the gravel parking lot because I would have fallen flat on my face otherwise. I felt relieved to see smooth asphalt approaching the door.

A security guard, a cute white man with a buzz haircut and physique reminiscent of an ex-military man, answered the door when

Money rang the bell. His tight V-neck T-shirt read "security" in large white letters, and his ripped chest protruded. He shook MMoney'shand firmly and let us in, but I noticed he kept staring at me as we left.

As soon as we walked in, we were greeted by a stunning waitress. She was topless, and even though her breasts were fake, they looked great. Her skin was gorgeous, and her smile was inviting. Money leaned down and kissed her on the cheek, looking at me like a piece of meat. Money then ordered us drinks and slapped her on the ass as she turned away.

I stood wondering where Money had taken me, wondering if this was a private party or a low-key tittie bar, and I stepped away from Money in an attempt to make sense of it all. I looked down the corridor and saw nothing, so all I could do was wonder when I heard a female laugh.

"Are you ready to have some fun?" Money asked as he approached me from behind, putting his strong arms around my waist.

I scowled in response, but he was unable to see it. ""f you are.""

The woman slowly closed the door, allowing me to peek inside, and I noticed one of the ball players from the other night laid back with his shirt off, being fed some grapes by another naked woman. What kind of place was this? As we crept down the corridor, a completely naked woman almost scared me half to death, standing in the doorway of a room. I jumped back into MMoney's arms, and he burst out laughing.

Money and I continued to stroll down the corridor, passing multiple rooms. Every room there had a different sound coming from the door. I heard laughter, moans, screams, music, and straight-out fucking noises. The lights down the corridor fucked with my eyes. The strobe light flickered like I was slowly walking through time. We reached the end of the corridor, and Money pulled on my arm to go right. I looked behind us and noticed more women prancing around in different costumes. I was dancing with so many weird images I saw before me.

I thought to myself," Is this nigga a V.I.P. member for this spot?" as Money took out his keys and opened the first door that we encountered.

When he opened the door, he saw two individuals watching the numerous cameras throughout the facility, a third counting money, and an elderly black woman sorting through cards that said "Fantasy Island." The Money was being thrown into red plastic tubs. Next, I focused on the cameras, which must have had over twenty rooms with various themes. I saw men on men, men dressed like babies, women being gang raped by three or four men, little people having sex, girls on girls, and anything else you could imagine. I became motionless, staring at all of this insane activity.

Money kissed the elderly black woman and said right, momma, keep up the good work." I find it strange that this fool works here with his mother.

I asked, sounding irate, "Money, what the fuck is this shit?" "his is among my most lucrative ventures." I asked, gesturing to the cameras," You mean you own this?"""" es! I earn slightly more than a million dollars a year from this club alone.""" "eally?"" I exclaimed in shock.

"his guy is an assistant to a congressman, and he spends roughly five stacks a month. He's a loyal customer. Oh, and this guy plays ball for Cleveland, and he comes in here after every home game. He spends roughly ten thousand a week here during the season."""" hoa! That means you're actually getting paid!" Indeed, there's no harm in realizing the deepest fantasies, is there?

I tried to think about it before responding, "m no, I guess.""""" o ahead and accompany me.""

Three.

Imagine

Now that you clearly understand who you are and what brings you joy, it's time to visualize the kind of life you want to lead with the appropriate woman and the steps necessary to get there.

Alright, so you've completed that. (I hope it was a good experience.) Let's look into what has to happen to make that happen.

It all comes down to balance. Hopefully, you already know what you want and what you have to offer. Now, you just need to focus on drawing a fairly accurate picture of the other person who can make it happen.

To determine a presence, it takes more than just punching in" – M = F" and balancing the equation" + F = H" (where M is you, F is her, and H is happiness).

The key is to imagine what you desire, place yourself in that situation, assess your role, and use the word "balance" to picture the kind of lady who would bring that about.

For instance, If you want to eat Italian food at least once a week and don't plan to learn how to make it, one of the things you'll be searching for in a woman is her willingness to prepare it for you. (Also, a woman is searching for a man who wants to enjoy her Italian cuisine.)

On all fronts, it starts with you identifying your objective, evaluating your contributions to the situation to make it happen, and speculating about the attributes the ideal woman might possess to realize it.

You mustn't overlook emotional and personality features while describing your ideal spouse. For example, if you are seeking someone nice and considerate,
& supportive, you need to note that somewhere when you find someone with contrary tendencies (demanding, hurtful, and vindictive), you can move on to a better option.

I cannot over-stress the importance of moving on when discovering someone is not what you need. It's about your happiness. (And to a certain extent, tthere'sas well.) If you wake up unhappy and unfulfilled every day and believe the person, you're with lies as the root.

Eventually, you're going to get angry. The other person is likely to feel just as unhappy and unfulfilled, and they will eventually become angry. It's best to avoid the unhappy and unfulfilled rut and find someone who you can be happy with and who can be happy with you.

"here is a person in the world who will love and appreciate everyone."

Theresa, women out there who would be thrilled to be with you, no matter how unusual you are or the kind of life you would like to lead. (The difficulty comes in when you want the woman who wants you. Ooooh. That sounds like a topic for another book.) This may sound like the kind of wisdom mothers have been telling their loveless children for years, but there is a preponderance of truth to it.

The added value

Although having good looks is important, keeping a man interested takes much more than that. "The man" must be drawn to you for other reasons if he wants to spend more time with you.

It's human nature to desire valuable goods; let's face it. Men are no different from women in that their first inclination would be to acquire something that they find extremely valuable in a store, provided they have the financial means to do so.

This idea, which has two interpretations, is highly significant in partnerships.

- Adding value to oneself.
- Enhancing the relationship with value.

You must find a means to portray yourself as valuable to 'the man'.

Recall our conversation on loving oneself. A healthy love for oneself is mostly dependent on having high self-esteem. If you want someone else to treat you well, you must learn to treat yourself with respect and value.

Exhibit elegance in both your demeanour and your interactions with others. Discover your "style" and own it.

Alternatively, you could attempt to enhance the relationship by offering assistance, particularly with his goals and aspirations. It might be about his current position, where he is, or it might be about his plans, where he is going.

Seek methods to encourage him and instil in his subconscious the idea that you would be there for him no matter what the cards life dealt.

Why should I have to do all the work, you ask? How would he respond to that? You undoubtedly purchased this book to learn how to persuade a man to commit. In a partnership, you should also have expectations for yourself. You should let him know if he is failing to live up to your expectations in any manner. You still have the right to fire him and move on to find someone else if he still doesn't live up to your standards.

The theory of the dead duck

I want to tell you about something at this point that I'll refer to as "the dead duck theory." It's an idea you won't find in other books, but it provides a clear explanation of what we are attempting to discuss. Give me a moment to clarify what I mean.

How would you feel if you went hunting? (I know you don't, but for the sake of argument, let's say you do while we work this out.) You go hunting, and somewhere along the way, you spot a dead duck. Are you going to bring it home?

I bet you won't.

The same is true for guys. By nature, men are hunters. Technological innovation has made living so easy that we don't need to hunt before we can eat - but guess what? Men still possess the innate need to hunt.

Why do certain men betray their attractive wives? You might say it was a lack of self-control, but it was also that hunting instinct. Maintaining his interest in you is the tricky part. You know how much we all enjoy a little mystery in our lives—it makes things so fascinating, doesn't it?

You like him, I know that. Don't collapse into his arms like a limp duck, even though he seems cool and collected. A dead duck is so unattractive that no one wants one. It's not worth much compared to something you found on your own.

No, I'm not suggesting you are game, but I think you see the comparison. When it's his turn to pursue you, don't hound him with phone calls and follow him about.

Alright, do you know someone who initiated contact and flopped like a dead duck?

I acknowledge that it occurs, and occasionally, things work out well for them, but the real question is: are you willing to take that chance? as that is how the cards are stacked against you?

-

#2 Addition of Value

Aim not to be a dullard. You are worth far more than that. Avoid collapsing into his arms, dead as a duck he failed to pursue. If he didn't feel the need for you and pursued the "chase" on his own, he wouldn't respect you as much.

Consider this: why is "playing hard to get" so effective? The message is that The Lady is a unique brand; everyone wants to be a part of it and get something unique. Now, be cautious not to overdo it if you decide to take this approach (playing hard to get). It's important to be "scarce" enough without appearing indifferent.

Recall that your thoughts have a great influence over your behaviour. You can show "the man" your value without proving it to him. Let him recognize the value in you by being authentic and self-assured.

How can you tell when you're losing your worth and feeling afraid?

- When you sacrifice your morals, sense of value, or health to appease a man.

You are setting yourself up for failure if you alter your values and beliefs in the relationship just because he asks you to rather than because you are persuaded.

A small amount of self-worth goes a long way,

Exhibit grace,

- Show encouragement,

- Acknowledge and validate him;

- Provide for each person's need for companionship.

1.3. What distinguishes sexual magnetism from sexual energy?

You need to be able to distinguish between sexual energy and sexual magnetism, for example. Although they are two distinct ideas, they are connected.

The real energy, the energy that passes through your body, is sexual. The projection of this sexual energy outward is known as sexual magnetism.

Even though you may be quite adept at controlling your sexual energy, you are not projecting any of it outward. Alternatively, you might portray a lovely exterior sexual image yet have a weak understanding of your inside energy.

Training from the Charisma School addresses both of these. Initially, focusing on the recognition and maturation of sexual energy, followed by its manifestation to generate sexual magnetism.

You must first sense the sexual energy that resides within your body. To become conscious of its movements, to clear the obstacles keeping the energy from flowing freely, and to enhance both the quantity and quality of sexual energy that enters your body.

People who naturally suppress their sexual energy eventually develop energetic, mental, emotional, and physical barriers that impede the flow of energy. The body is preventing the energy from moving freely. Blocks and resistances prevent it from moving as efficiently as possible. You can have obstacles in your sexual energy, nevertheless, and not experience sexual dysfunction. Perhaps psychological issues are limited to seduction. A good seduction requires an unrestricted flow of sexual energy throughout the whole process, as numerous seducers have learned over the millennia. It needs to be given room to spread. Restricting it makes it far more difficult for the seduction to progress organically. These barriers are frequently the source of awkwardness, shyness, nervousness, and a lack of ideas on what to say. Untying these knots, letting the sexual energy flow freely, and finding comfort in it should, therefore, be your top priorities. You cannot emit sexual energy or become magnetic if you are not completely at ease with it.

You become capable of externalizing sexual energy when you can experience it and feel at ease with it. This is the allure of sex. You generate some kind of sexual effect and allow people around you to sense your sexual energy.

It is possible to enhance one's overall sexual magnetism, or the capacity to consistently radiate this energy without making a deliberate attempt. Alternatively, you may create strategies for sniper-like laser-targeted interventions. To actively seduce someone, you employ several methods to arouse their sexual desire.

Both are efficient at their jobs. Generally speaking, I advise developing a broad sexual magnetism. It is usually a very organic approach. Nevertheless, even without projection techniques, isn't sexual energy felt? Why can't you just experience sexual energy and go on? Your particular obstacles will determine the answer to that question. If your sources of external projection are unobstructed, you will inherently project sexual energy and possess a high sexual magnetism. However, if you haven't observed a strong sexual magnetism up until now, you probably do have external sources of projection blockages that need to be addressed and trained. Even so, raising your level of attractiveness can already be achieved by simply becoming aware of and cultivating your sexual energy. You will unavoidably release some of this energy into the outer world if you can recognize, explore, and let it flow freely within yourself. But frequently, this might not be sufficient. Training in sexual magnetism is, therefore, necessary. It is possible to attain a significantly higher level of energy externalization and mastery over your personal energy projection.

5. INSIDE THE GAME

INTERNAL GAME: RULES TEN

I recall the first evening I spent with Mr H, following his directive to "talk to anyone", as I had spent the entire day aimlessly strolling about the city. I was excited to finally meet him in person and was ready to hurl all my issues at him, knowing he would find a quick solution. I recall seeing him go through the hotel entrance.

We started talking once he sat in the armchair in front of me. As we spoke, I became more and more certain that I had, at last, discovered the person who would assist me in getting my revenge on all those people—the well-liked and superficial leaders, specifically—who, in my opinion, weren't deserving of having successful lives.

"Why are you here?" he said, and I replied,

"I am here because I want to go back to my city as the Count of Montecristo! I want to SHOW all those stupid superficial idiots that hang out with the coolest girls, that I am in charge. I want to be respected!"

Mr. H gave me a look that, at the time, I couldn't interpret and said:

"What the fuck are you talking about? Montecristo doesn't exist, you are Montecristo."

In case you were unaware, Alexandre Dumas wrote The Count of Montecristo in 1845. It tells the story of Edmond Dantès, a man who was betrayed by friends and imprisoned for over ten years until being declared dead after being accused of a murder he did not commit. In the cell, he encounters a monk who discloses that he is very rich and has hidden a fortune on the island of Montecristo. After escaping the jail and discovering the treasure, Dantès returns home using the fictitious name Count of Montecristo. None of his foes knew who he was, so the Count exacted revenge on them all.

Why did Mr. H tell me that now? Since this is the first rule of the Inner Game, keep in mind that Montecristo is a symbol of taking retribution on others and of "doing things" for others.

N. Rule 1. MONTECRISTO IS NOT REAL!

Whatever you do in life, whether wooing a woman or making money, DO IT ONLY FOR YOURSELF AND NOT FOR ANYONE ELSE.

The outcomes and, most importantly, THE RESPECT will come when you set aside your grudge or need to prove yourself, thus calming your spirit.

To compensate for insecurity, trying hard is an unnatural manifestation of fake greatness, often ONLY WITH THE WORDS. Remember that trying hard DOESN'T MEAN DEMONSTRATING. The demonstration is the natural consequence of your actions, determined by a positive attitude and a dominant mentality in the form of CONCRETE ACTIONS. NEVER TAKE PRIDE IN ANYTHING!

N. Rule 2. Your worst enemy is your ego!

EGO: What is it? The notorious and imperceptible inner voice known as the ego is what essentially wrecks people's lives. Your false self-image, fueled by an excessive idealization of who you are and what you believe others perceive you to be, is known as your ego.

The ego is like a mask; it shields you from your shortcomings by constantly placing the blame elsewhere or by inventing several justifications for putting off solving issues.

For instance, imagine yourself heading to work while strolling along the street. All of a sudden, you spot a female walking by. She's your dream girlfriend—beautiful, with an amazing body and eyes that will blow your mind! Though your inner voice starts to tell you that you might be late for work, that she might be rushing and not want to listen, or that the girl in question has physical flaws (being too high or too low, blonde instead of brunette, etc.) to find an excuse not to go talk to her, you still want to go talk to her.

Chapter Eight

Beth immersed herself in her job the following day. How had her life gotten so complicated all of a sudden? Yes, exactly. It was Lord Langston again. What about this man caused her to get into problems and doubt her choices? She was happy. She was content. Or she would be once she found a means to look after Mr. Jones. She thought about the debt constantly. She became insane since her mother didn't appear to care. Was she blind to the danger?

"You are going to sand a hole right into that wood, Beth, if you aren't careful," Sally whispered from behind her.

She continued to sand. "Before I can make it look like marble, it has to be smooth."

"No one in the audience will be able to tell, love."

At Sally's slight reprimand, Beth paused and closed her eyes. She landed on the chilly ground. "You're right, as always," she said, tossing the sandpaper aside and wiping her hands.

Would you like to discuss the events of yesterday night? You were gone when I last saw you during the first act.

Beth looked up at Sally. "You were exceptionally intelligent."

Sally extended Beth a hand. "You can't sit on the floor and talk to me."

Beth gave in and let herself be hauled to her feet. She brushed her clothes free of sanding dust. Is it an improvement?"

Yes, but if you were so fond of the play, then why did you leave? After that, I was excited to spend time with you.

Beth trailed Sally to a group of seats in the corner of the spacious set area. Sally looked gorgeous today in a light blue morning dress. Beth wore an apron and her worn-out brown wool clothing. Her hands were dusty and rough from working on the smaller elements of the set, and the apron was stained with paint. Approaching the box was Lord Langston. However, you already know if you spoke with Mr. St. Clair last night.

She would not look at Sally. "He may have mentioned going to see the play with my best friend."

Beth smiled back at her. "He's really attractive, Mr. St. Clair."

"He had nothing but good things to say about you, Beth," Sally smiled. "How did he phrase it? Yes, any girl who has the confidence to confront Langston has gained his admiration.

Sally's laughing eyes met Beth's. "Seeing him was much harder than I had anticipated. Mother, of course, only made matters worse. She whined during the first act until I was about to scream, at which point she insisted on our departure before intermission. When Langston arrived, I had gone outside to look for Mr. Carter so he could turn the carriage around. Mother embraced his offer to see us home as though God had personally sent the message.

Sally chuckled. She probably did. She desires that you get settled.

She desires for us to be saved from poverty by a wealthy man. I can get that she misses her former life, but we can't go back," Beth said, her tone turning contemptuous. "My mother persistently mentions that I allowed a marquis to elude my control."

"Honestly, if he were chasing me instead of St. Clair, I might have to think about becoming his mistress. One day, the man will become a duke.

"Sally!"

Sally winked at her. "How horrible could it be to let a man like that know you're at home?" Beth, you had to feel something. You previously had love for him.

Picking at the dried paint on her apron, Beth glanced down at her lap. "Sally, I can't stay in the past. I cannot regret taking that road because it only leads to regret. I valued that time far too much. However, our paths have now diverged. I'm content with my life.

Sally looked at her for a long while. "What was your mother's reaction to having Langston at her disposal?"

"She still thinks I can catch him like a fish and reel him in."

Sally chuckled. Beth, he's a really lovely fish. It may get worse.

Beth glared at her pal. "He is unable to wed me. I'm a painter in a theatre. His dad will never consent to it. People would avoid us in society. It would be the beginning of a catastrophe. Our relationship began years ago when we were young and foolish. I can't count on him to uphold it.

One of the workers entered the spacious warehouse and called Sally's name as she leaned forward, prepared to speak.

"Miss Bishop? For you, a letter

Beth got up to greet the workman, glancing at Sally. She quickly looked at the letter with her name in bold, male handwriting across the front. Returning to Sally, she pushed her finger under the seal. She unfolded it and took a quick look at what was inside. "The man is unyielding in his demands."

Sally smiled and got up out of the chair. "I assume that's Lord Langston's note."

"It's a summons to the Royal Academy," Beth said, letting go of the letter.

Bending over, Sally took up the message. She immediately skimmed over the contents and grinned. "This is good. Langston is hoping to meet you. Despite his tendency toward conceit, I admire his tenacity.

Beth settled into a chair. "This is not something I can do. I refuse to allow him to shatter my heart again.

Sally gripped her hand. Beth, our hearts are open to change. He would not have reached out if he didn't care.

"It's guilt,"

"What is the reason for his guilt?"

Beth returned Sally's inquiring look with a slick one of her own. Sally was the next to fall into the chair.

Is your mum aware of this? Sally muttered.

Beth chuckled. You behave as though my loss of virginity is a top-secret matter. No, Mom is not aware of it. Only you and Langston are aware of it. A soul cannot be told.

"That idiot! To abandon you in that manner after... following..."

It wasn't like that, Sally. His mom was not well. All he could do was go see her.

"What if you had a child with you?"

Beth closed her eyes. Numerous things had the potential to go wrong, yet they didn't. "That things transpired as they did was a godsend. His mother needed him. My dad required me. My mother needed me. She still does.

"Beth, what about you? What about the necessities for you?"

Beth put a grin on her face. "What I need is not important right now." She took the letter from Sally, folded it back up, and placed it into her pocket. "I ought to go back to work,"

"Are you going to see him, or not?"

Beth gave a headshake. "What would the purpose be?"

"I'm not sure? Make amends? Allow him to assist you?"

With sorrow engulfing the corners of her heart, Beth shook her head. "Neither Langston nor I can undo the past."

However, it could imply that the painting will be on display. You have this dream.

"Sally, dreams are for kids. Both of us are aware of that.

Beth scooped up the sandpaper and walked back to her workspace. She tested the raw wood's smoothness by feeling it with her hand after rubbing the paper over it. She felt calmed by the actions repeated. She heard Sally leave her alone and enter the large storage area.

It was probably for the best that she was growing accustomed to her alone time. She was only 25 years old. She had a long day of being by herself ahead of her.

Could I just say something, Miss Bishop?"

Randal Alderman. This was not a conversation she had been looking forward to. After setting the sandpaper on the ground, she stood up. "Sir, good morning."

A BETTER PARTNER FOR HIS OR HER PLEASURE

Let me help you find the ideal arrangement so that the G-Spot and He-Spot work well for you and your partner before we dive headfirst into indulging your partner's Spots.

Her: Tell her all the flattering things you know she enjoys hearing, such as how gorgeous and seductive she is and what you would love to do to those traits. You may arrange a rather straightforward, reasonably priced surprise for her.

His: Heighten him and his imagination by throwing a simple " I'm not putting anything on inside" where he can't necessarily do much to you; he'll drive home wild to you.

Her: Caress her neck, ears, and back with a gentle touch, then carefully undress her while planting passionate kisses on her thighs, toes, and neck.

His: Make him change his fantasies by acting out small role-plays, saying the appropriate things, and gently stroking him before undressing.

Her: Gently stroking and feeling her hair. Pull her neck back, gaze at her vulnerable nude body, show it reverence, bend down, and kiss her stomach, waist, and thighs while holding her ass (believe me, ladies adore it).

His: Give him a quick kiss on the ears, tease and caress his nipples, take his hands and massage every part of your body, feeling especially tender areas. Don't forget to show him how you feel, but maintain your control by keeping him motionless.

Her: Give her a passionate kiss, hitting all the places she loves to be kissed. Feel, play, and kiss every part of her body. Rub and use your penis to caress her entire body. Lightly touch her vagina with your penis tip at first, then deeper strokes (without penetrations yet).

His: Ring his penis with your finger and stroke in accordance, massage his butt, and caress his extremely sensitive balls.

Her: Give her another passionate kiss, then pull her in close to find her G-Spot. She should feel your warmth as you prepare to reach and place her hands over her head.

His: Reach out to locate his He-Spot following a satisfying penis play.

Putting down your hands

Your fingers? You must use all ten of them, the magic those tips pull. The gentle, warm, energetic, always prepared, and never-need-a-recharge advice that may drive them insane. At Your Fingertips! Use it to play, touch, and massage your entire body. Acquire the proper movements and strokes to make your partner angry.

LET US FIND HER

The G-spot—a well-lubricated finger—into the vagina travelling upward—is said to be difficult to find, or perhaps you're not performing your job properly. Do you receive a rough, bumpy feeling similar to the roof of the inner mouth when you bend your finger(s) towards the abdomen from the inside? True? It's here!

Have you not? Spend extra time practising foreplay, then give it another go later. At this point, the G-Spot is starting to show itself, and the female body is tingling with desire.

Section Two

The Alluring Method

Most of us know that there are certain things we may do to make the person we want to seduce us more comfortable and tempt them. The problem is that we are typically too self-centred, thinking more about what we want from other people than what they might want from us. Sometimes, we do something attractive, but because we're rushing to get what we want, we often follow it up with something selfish or aggressive; other times, we act without thinking and show a mundane and petty side of ourselves, shattering anyone's illusions or fantasies they may have about us. Seldom do our attempts at seduction last long enough to make a big difference.

You can't draw someone in only by depending on your seductive nature or by occasionally acting in a way that appeals to others. Seduction is a slow process; the more time you take and the slower you proceed, the more deeply you will pierce the mind of your target. It's a skill that requires focus, patience, and strategic thought. You must always be one step ahead of your opponent, putting a spell on them, making them look foolish, and scattering dust in their eyes.

These techniques let you get outside your mentality and into your victim's, enabling you to use it as an instrument. The chapters are grouped inexplicably, beginning with your initial contact with your victim and concluding with your last conversation with them. The foundation of this order's success is a body of universal laws. Psychology of people: You can't initiate a seduction until you've addressed your everyday anxieties and phobias since others are naturally drawn to them. You gently ease their worries and divert their otherwise busy thoughts.

I've got you on my mind. You will find assistance in this quest in the first few chapters. Individuals in relationships naturally tend to become unduly familiar with one another. Their interactions with each other led to a state of boredom and stagnation. Mysteriousness is the essence of seduction; to maintain it, you must continually astonish, excite, and even surprise your target. A seduction should never become acclimated to a routine. You will learn how to alternate between pleasure and pain, hope and despair until your victims weaken and give up in the middle and latter chapters. In every instance, one tactic prepares the way for the next, enabling you to take it further with an even riskier and more violent move. A seducer is neither timid nor gentle.

To assist you in moving through the seduction process, the chapters are organized into four stages: luring the victim into thinking about you; opening their emotional channels by evoking moments of pleasure and confusion; delving deeper by activating repressed desires and working on their unconscious; and, lastly, causing them to physically surrender. (Each stage has a brief introduction, labelling, and description.) If you follow these phases, you can work on your victim's psyche more successfully and create a ritual's slow, hypnotic beat. In actuality, the process of seduction can be seen as an initiation rite when individuals are taken out of their comfort zones, exposed to novel situations, and put through trials to usher them into a new life.

It is advised that you review each chapter to ensure you are learning as much as possible. When applying these techniques, you should carefully consider which ones are best for your particular victim; a handful may be sufficient, depending on the complexity of your victim's issues and the degree of resistance you face. These techniques apply to both social and political seductions, except the sexual element in Phase Four.

Steer clear of the urge to improvise or to wrap up your seduction too quickly. You're being conceited rather than seductive. In today's fast-paced and impromptu world, you must make an impression.

If you take your time and honour the seduction process, you will not only break through your victim's resistance but also make them fall in love.

You can't draw someone in only by depending on your seductive nature or by occasionally acting in a way that appeals to others.

Seduction is a slow process; the more time you take and the slower you proceed, the more deeply you will pierce the mind of your target.

It's a skill that requires focus, patience, and strategic thought.

You must always be one step ahead of your opponent, putting a spell on them, making them look foolish, and scattering dust in their eyes.

The chapters are broken down into four phases to help you progress the seduction: gaining emotional access to the victim by inciting moments of pleasure and confusion, delving deeper by activating buried impulses in their unconscious, and finally, inducing physical submission.

Steer clear of the urge to improvise or to wrap up your seduction too quickly. You're being conceited rather than seductive. Because daily life is hectic and impromptu, you have to offer something special.

Section Three: The Pursuit

The Tale of Love

Maria had finally decided to phone Bruce. She said aloud, "I'll call him after gym in the morning." "No! How am I thinking? It's much too early! I'll finish it with my girls after lunch. No, no, no. He might be out with his friends this weekend. Alright, take a deep breath.

She closed her eyes, inhaled deeply, and then let out an elegant exhale. She said aloud, "I'll call him after I visit Mum and take Pooch for a walk," then paused. Oh, please, I must unwind. Just the thought of calling him is driving me mad. I'm obsessed with this guy, even though I don't know him. Alright, I have to take a deep breath. It's time for a cold shower!

The Hunter

When you are the one pursuing, you can unexpectedly alter the course of events, while the target of your desire lacks inspiration and motivation. The change you want to see has to be bold, tempting, exquisite, forceful, challenging, and unexpected. Before you make contact, hone your art of seduction and then make adjustments to achieve the desired outcome.

Be aware of your precarious situation; the pursuer's position is helpless and uncomfortable, and it takes work, persistence, patience, and the ability to swallow your pride. It can be a stressful and challenging internal battle to get the approach correct, and it could even lead you to undermine your achievement. However, you can overcome it if you rewire your brain and alter your patterns.

The Ideal

The individual you want is in a position to make the decision. While you make all the effort, they experience comfort, power, and control. All they have to do is say yes or no.

They feel proud of their ease, control, and power. They are susceptible to your surprises and alterations because of their pride. You will be able to take away their sensation of control and power and make them uncomfortable if your sensual rhythm and deft adjustments are on the spot.

A Seduction Win

When a pursuer approaches someone they want to date, they should make them feel uncomfortable and inspire positive feelings and thoughts, making them seem valued and appealing.

Never push yourself too hard.

Recall that subtlety is the essence of flirting; going overboard would make it impossible for you to win him over. Suppose you ever go so far as to come out with outrageous pick-up lines and make openly sexual remarks. In that case, you will never gain the desired attention, especially if the other person is uncomfortable.

Never lower yourself to a lower level.

Laughing at his jokes is a wonderful idea, but only after he's truly said something humorous. You'll come across as precisely that if you laugh foolishly at everything he says. Don't forget to be gentle when offering compliments. Giving him small praises is acceptable, but you should never put him in an elevated position. Remember, it's okay to express your appreciation for your partner, but keep it in check—after all, he's not exactly Tom Hiddleston. Remember that it's crucial to conduct appropriately for your age. You should behave like a mature, full-grown woman; don't put up a cutesy, infantile front because it won't work. You wouldn't want to touch a guy with a ten-foot pole if he's like the entire juvenile sort, girl.

Never let yourself get down on yourself.

Please refrain from being little yourself. Never put yourself down in a conversation with someone you're interested in. Speaking poorly of oneself conveys to him the impression that you lack self-respect, which is never acceptable.

You should never behave rudely.

When it comes to flirting, a little sarcasm and a lot of comedy are fantastic. But you should never let things get out of hand or permit yourself to sound harsh. Playfully making fun of someone can make a huge difference from treating them badly, so watch how you behave.

Never tell lies.

This is true in all facets of life, not only flirtation, and you should never misrepresent your identity. It is rude and terrible to fabricate fake facts about oneself and drag someone along. You should also refrain from lying "for his benefit." Pretending to be someone else's attraction is never a good idea.

You should never speak too much.

Whether you're flirting or not, you should be mindful not to take up too much of the discussion when you're with someone. Remember that having a discussion requires two individuals to participate, as it is a two-way street. In addition to making him lose interest in you, if you continue talking without allowing him to speak, you will irritate everyone, regardless of gender.

It is never appropriate to discuss gloomy topics.

Speaking of talking, you should avoid delicate subjects while brainstorming conversation starters. You shouldn't bring up your ex. After all, would you want your partner to bring up his? Not in my opinion! If you've only recently gotten to know one another better, you should also refrain from sharing too much personal information. You also want to steer clear of political and religiously charged topics.

Never try to play too hard to win.

Alright. I feel like I should reiterate how stupid guys are when taking cues—and I mean that in the kindest manner imaginable. They have no idea what we're talking about, even when we're telling them straight. Playing games with a man is never a smart idea because males aren't usually the most understanding when it comes to someone else's feelings.

Many men might feel uncomfortable approaching a stunning woman and discussing with her. Most of the time, guys are inclined to use cliched methods of flattery, such as telling the woman she is attractive. Sadly, this strategy rarely succeeds and can have disastrous results. In addition to being cliched and clichéd, it suggests that the man ranks higher on some kind of "totem pole," devaluing him and making him seem unworthy of her attention.

As an alternative, some men might try "negging," which is a tactic that entails complimenting a woman behind her back or making an inconsiderate remark about how she looks in an attempt to "trickle" her into submission. This strategy is both unsuccessful and disrespectful; it gives the impression that the male lacks confidence in his ability to detect dishonesty and disrespect her.

Real interest in a lady's personality and appearance is the secret to effective conversation with any woman. Consider her sense of style, sense of humour, distinctive tattoos or wardrobe pieces, or even something as basic as an intriguing phrase on a t-shirt instead of concentrating only on her physical characteristics, such as her long legs or manicures. Sincerely valuing these attributes will demonstrate your desire to learn more about her personality before pursuing a sexual relationship with her.

Women are also particularly adept at reading nonverbal clues, so it's not difficult to figure out whether someone is interacting with them with a hidden agenda. Men should understand that showing sincere curiosity and learning more about themselves than just their physical appearance can build deeper relationships in which both people feel valued and accepted for who they are.

Section Six

A self-assured and gifted man can have a strong pull on women. However, there are four possible outcomes if you approach a pretty woman and mumble something she can't comprehend. First, she might ask you to repeat what you said, putting her on the defensive and causing her to feel uneasy. Your body language might also impact the scenario; if you seem to be acting slyly or surreptitiously around her, she will probably feel uncomfortable around you. Thirdly, your mumbled speech may be too distorted for her to understand, which will not make a positive impression. The fourth and final possibility is that everyone is too busy trying to get away from you to notice your awkward effort at conversation!

To make her think of you as an alpha male worthy of chatting with, you must act and speak with competence and value while approaching her during the day. When approaching her on the sidewalk, step in front of her and smile firmly but softly. Use a volume that shows you are comfortable with your actions without being overbearing. This will demonstrate your courage and confidence in front of others. Walking alongside her will give the impression that she is in control.

However, we must avoid speaking too rapidly or increasing our tone higher than usual during these situations because the adrenaline surge brought on by anxiousness or worry will work against us and prevent the desired result. To properly project confidence, we must ensure that we deliver at a slower pace and with a deeper pitch than usual to avert such incidents. Additionally, this will enable us to speak with greater semantic richness, providing more information about ourselves and adding value for possible discussion partners while maintaining a level of composure that will allow them to clearly understand everything we are saying.

An intentional pause is one of the most effective techniques to talk effectively. You can make an immensely strong statement by pausing between your lines and letting the audience fill in the blanks with their ideas and feelings. By pausing, you give a kind of fuel to your fire that makes the people listening feel even more intensely. Consider, for illustration, making two distinct approaches to a person you encounter on the street: one without a pause and one with. Without a pause, the statement "Hey, I saw you crossing the street just now, and I noticed something about you" may not seem very amazing; nevertheless, when it is followed by a little pause and the statement "You have the coolest jeans I ever saw," it becomes much more powerful.

During silence, listeners can use their imaginations to fill in the blank with their ideas or guesses. This makes them eager about what might be said next and makes them unintentionally try to guess. They are forced out of their comfort zones while feeling intrigued and more likely to accept and remember whatever comes next. This produces a sort of mental judo where they must come up with potential replies or remarks before being presented with them.

Speaking in silence has additional advantages. It has an innately captivating aspect that, when employed skillfully, may captivate listeners by involving them emotionally and cognitively. Furthermore, pauses can also be used to show competence. Taking deliberate intervals can show respect for the people listening to you and confidence in your thoughts, as opposed to speaking hastily or rushing through sentences to finish them faster, which may signal inexperience. Allowing yourself to take deep breaths between ideas will guarantee that your words are always understood effectively and avoid any lack of focus or momentum. Using pauses tactfully throughout speeches or presentations can prove to be important.

To sum up, pausing in talks or other oral communication is a highly useful technique you should never undervalue. It lets you create tension while maintaining your confidence and shows consideration for the listening people. Furthermore, it conveys an air of authority and engages listeners on several levels, making pauses essential to effective public speaking.

Body language is one of the most crucial elements of any good conversation with a possible love partner. Since body language makes up a big portion of communication, it is crucial to understand it to express your thoughts and sentiments clearly. Pay close attention to your body language when approaching someone you like. Even when we try to disguise our genuine feelings, our bodies frequently show them. Pay attention to how you appear and behave to avoid making the other person feel nervous or uncomfortable.

Particularly, the feet may reveal a lot about our emotions: pointing them in the direction of someone usually means that we want to be closer while pointing them in the opposite direction suggests that we might be thinking about something else. Crossing one's arms or legs can be interpreted as a gesture of comfort, suggesting that the subconscious has decided there's no need to get ready to leave the conversation. Other cues, like lying, include scratching one's nose or ears. When under stress, the brain triggers erectile tissue in these regions, causing us to touch them instinctively.

Speaking with someone else requires you to also modify your vocal intonation appropriately. Use pauses and dramatic inflexions to communicate confidence and authority while speaking clearly and slowly.

Adopt a "take it or leave it" mentality; avoid becoming overly invested in the result or anxious to be accepted; remain calm and foster a relaxing environment for all parties. Not only should you be aware of your body language, but you also pay attention to what you say, as words make up only 7% of communication, yet they still impact the impression you leave behind.

Finally, try taking the lead instead of following their cues when engaging with someone you've never met. If they're already strolling somewhere else, ask them to stop and talk with you! Aim for mystery by inventing phoney deadlines that imply you were also wanted somewhere else by other people. This will create a sense of intrigue and help them stay focused on you!

Time Management

Acquire Strategies For Effectively Managing Time As A Writer And Elevate Your Position On The Renowned Writers' Ranking

(A Comprehensive Manual For Achieving Academic Excellence And Well-rounded Development)

Norris Morrison

Never give up on your goals:

Goals, as previously indicated, are a simple way to monitor your time and effort. As a result, you must occasionally push yourself. Never assume that just because you've reached a certain goal, it's okay to take a nap. Establish new objectives that are consistent with your long-term objectives after completing a previous set of goals. Your time and efforts will always be put to good use in this way. This is not meant to turn you into a machine that works nonstop without any breaks. You must schedule time and make a goal out of relaxing, even if that's what you want to do. This will guarantee that you don't waste time on unscheduled tasks, as this is likely one of the ways you'll wind up doing something that drags on for far too long. For example, if you don't make it a goal to sleep from 9:00 p.m. to 6:00 a.m., you'll likely have no restrictions about what you can and cannot accomplish during this time. You may watch a movie till midnight or wake up at seven in the morning. If you really want to cultivate the habit of completing the tasks you set for yourself, don't only establish objectives for the days you want to manage your time efficiently. Set goals on a regular basis.

Having seen the several facets of goal setting, you will be more equipped to understand the role that goals play in time management when I discuss it in the later sections of this book.

Completing Tasks

Another time management strategy that productivity consultant David Allen uncovered is getting things done. The GTD method is the well-known name for this approach. This strategy requires us to put the significant chores and initiatives we have planned in our minds on paper. Put differently, it is transferring our thoughts from within our heads to a physical medium, such as a diary or notepad. The next step would be to divide these undertakings into more manageable, achievable goals after writing them down in a notepad.

Our memory is capable of recalling. Nevertheless, when we are working quickly or under a lot of pressure, this ability will not serve us well. We must be careful not to commit too much to memory in order to prevent this, especially when it comes to crucial deliverables. It will, therefore, be simple to find them and concentrate on them if you write them down somewhere. To do these activities, this focus is necessary.

The ideology underlying GTD

David Allen claims that there are two fundamental components to this strategy: perspective and control. This approach suggests a specific workflow procedure that may be utilised to manage all of the obligations and tasks one wants to complete within a predetermined amount of time. The basic idea of this method is to write down all of our objectives and get them out of our heads. This is because, in his opinion, when a person's mind is clear of clutter, they can concentrate and think more clearly. If he has some degree of mental clarity, he will be better equipped to make decisions. It takes mental clarity to concentrate on the following six elements:

✓ Present activities: These are things that must be finished right away. This can be as easy as getting ready for the meeting that is due to start in an hour. Put otherwise, these are the assignments that you have scheduled for the next few hours. You can see that these are incredibly short-term objectives.

✏ Current projects: The short-term initiatives you are involved in are what constitute current projects. For example, you might be involved in this neighbourhood effort that entails Christmas street decorating. These, too, are transient and need your regular care.

✏ Areas of Responsibility: These can be long-term or short-term responsibilities. The important thing to remember in this situation is to concentrate on the immediate obligations, or more accurately, the daily tasks that need to be completed. For example, as a student, you must complete your daily homework assignments and dedicate yourself to learning.

✏ Goals for the next one to two years: These are objectives that can be completed in that time frame. This is the point at which daily tasks give way to somewhat more ambitious objectives. Losing thirty pounds in a year is an example of a goal that fits into this category.

✓ Three to five-year life goals: After deciding on your objectives for the upcoming year, it's time to concentrate on your goals for the following three to five years. These are longer-term objectives. Therefore, preparation should begin now. For instance, you might want to buy a specific car within three years. You must begin saving money for that car today if you want to acquire it in three years.

✏ Long-term life objectives: As the name implies, these are long-term objectives. Following the completion of your other goals, you will be better able to determine your long-term objectives and where you want to go in life. This clarity will improve your long-term objectives. These objectives typically have a longer timeline than five years. If you are a student, one example of this objective might be to make career plans. If you currently hold a job, you can begin saving and making plans for your retirement. In order to accomplish these goals in the long run, some action must also be taken now.

The top-down method is typically the subject of most theories. All that the top-down technique entails is concentrating on the long-term objective and dissecting it into multiple smaller, more manageable objectives. But, this strategy is based on the bottoms-up methodology. This is because, in Allen's opinion, not everyone is able to concentrate, see the wider picture, or set long-term objectives, particularly when they are constantly finding it difficult to do their daily tasks. This is a lost opportunity to practise concentration and set long-term objectives, particularly if you do not influence your present situation. An individual will have the time and clarity to consider the wider picture when he assumes responsibility for the duties or commitments scheduled for the day. Therefore, the main goal of this approach is to complete tasks quickly so that the person can concentrate on longer-term goals.

His approach recommends reviewing the situation once a week. We often get a fresh perspective while examining our accomplishments and objectives, and this new viewpoint should be utilised to determine our priorities for the next week. Setting the scene for these weekly evaluations is crucial. It won't work to just review the list of tasks accomplished. Sort related tasks together; for instance, you may group all of your weekly meetings while categorising all of your phone calls separately. This will enable us to appropriately review the tasks that have been accomplished.

The GTD technique suggests keeping track of, organising and accessing data about the obligations and tasks that need to be fulfilled.

When we don't have enough time to plan, we frequently experience mental obstacles. For this reason, we shouldn't depend too much on our brains' ability to remember things. This approach tries to deal with these problems and offers a productive way to write down your objectives and periodically examine them.

Having organisational abilities is vital in life. This could entail tidying the home, filing documents at work, or even making sure the cupboard is arranged with spices. These are all basic yet very important organising habits. You'll find that once you establish the habit, it comes naturally to you.

Life organisation is more difficult than one might imagine. You see, there are limits and boundaries that you must be able to overcome. You must be able to establish objectives and see through to completion. It takes patience and hard work to be organised. Do you feel up to the task?

These practice exercises for organisation are provided.

1) Enter your kitchen and search through the cabinets. Do you notice the assortment of soups, junk food, and/or spices? Are they placed neatly or in disarray? They are probably messy since we don't have time to put our food in a nice order because we have so much on our plates. But congratulations if your cupboard is organised well! Now put your cabinet in order and time how long it takes. What was the duration of the process? I doubt it would be very long. This activity was designed to demonstrate to you that while organising your cabinet is simple, organising your thoughts requires patience. This was also meant to demonstrate the negative effects of having an untidy kitchen or cabinet. You probably didn't believe it could.

2) Please proceed to your wardrobe now. Choose the location where the clothing is

folded into drawers rather than on hooks. Do these outfits follow any particular pattern at all now? Unfortunately, I doubt that there is a trend. Please pull out and arrange all of your clothes from the drawer. Choose a pattern for the organisation, then follow it through. The garments could be arranged according to colour, style, or even personal taste. This experiment was designed to demonstrate once more how your mind can be impacted by messy things in your life.

3) I want you to go look at every shoe you have. If you have a lot, that is. I can complete this task with ease because I have quite a few. Anyway, take another look at your shoes and try to identify any patterns. Have you noticed any trends? Not at all? Not quite a shocker, actually. We tend to underestimate how disorganised we actually are. So again, I want you to arrange your shoes according to some kind of pattern.

The pattern may be based on preferences, size, colour, or style.

These were simply a few easy practice exercises for the organisation. I hope you understood the general idea I was attempting to convey to you. To put it plainly, we lack organisation. We must be. Examine your life and yourself, and consider how you might make it better. Consider how you can better organise and manage your time.

Even if these exercises show that getting more organised doesn't have to be that hard, we just aren't organised. If we're disorganised, how can we see our friends and family and better manage our time? Easy. We are unable to.

To better manage our time and ourselves, we must be organised. I believe we owe it to ourselves.

The following chapter will cover a few key points regarding time that you should never forget. We will discuss several approaches to acceptance and address the myth that time is overwhelming. Time is something you can better manage and control. Do not allow the false impression to govern you.

Are you prepared for the upcoming chapter?

Advice for Outsourcing and Delegating

Building your team requires careful consideration of a number of factors as well as the implementation of a few key tasks. To get you started, consider the following seven suggestions for efficient delegation.

Examine Your Needs.

Get a clear picture of what needs to be done before deciding what to delegate and to whom. This relates to monitoring your time usage and determining whether or not it is efficient. You might be shocked to see where your time is going and what is taking up your time if you take the time to monitor your daily activities.

2) Examine your choices.

Delegation can take many different forms, and the best one for you will depend on your requirements. The two most typical ones are:

a) Employ someone.

Hire a self-employed contractor.

3) Keep meticulous records.

The first step in outsourcing or delegating some of your work is to monitor the items that are essential to the smooth operation of your business or life. This could be a difficult step because, more often than not, you merely happen to think about this knowledge. Nonetheless, knowing this information will assist you in determining what tasks you should continue doing on your own and what you may assign.

4) Give assignments a priority.

You must decide on your delegation priorities and how you will assign, monitor, and oversee the work you delegate when you have everything recorded. A framework is in place to communicate information about what needs to be done.

Is this something that has to be finished immediately?

b) Can someone else complete this task, or do I have to?

5. Make use of technology.

Of course, there are moments when technology can be annoying, but it can also simplify work delegation and support you and your team in overcoming obstacles. Technology can help every member of your team, whether it is for file sharing, online training, or scheduling. Additionally, technology makes it possible to assemble a team of people in different places while giving the impression that everyone is seated in the same room.

6) Talk to each other.

For any kind of team, communication is crucial. In the end, without communication, you're just a group of people going about your own business that doesn't really serve anyone but yourself. You're not really a team. Making sure that everyone has access to the information and communicating in a clear, concise, and consistent manner are essential when delegating.

7) Establish confidence.

Trust is one of the most crucial components of delegation. This is reciprocal. You have to have faith that your team will finish the duties given to them, that you're giving them all the knowledge they need to execute this work and that you'll be available to them when they need it. The following are some strategies for building trust:

Respect one another.

c) Pay attention to what other people are saying.

d) Pay attention to constant communication.

d) Make commitments and follow through on them.

f) Consistency in honesty is key.

Delegating well is a terrific time management strategy, particularly if you're feeling overburdened by the amount of work you need to get done. You'll have more time to do the things you enjoy rather than spending all of your time on the things you have to do if you take the time to learn and implement these delegation tactics.

Professionals' Guide to Time Management

Professionals are aware of the influence time management abilities may have on their social lives and careers, just like students and parents do. Critical assignments, last-minute meetings, and team or managerial projects frequently cause them stress. Even if they are aware of the fundamentals of time management, they still need to be just as disciplined and dedicated to avoid getting sidetracked or finding an excuse to put off doing their job, which will only cause them to worry as they jam as much work as possible and lower the quality of their output. Any professional, regardless of degree or occupation, can improve their time management using the five suggestions listed below.

1. Set aside at least twenty minutes each day to organize and monitor your daily objectives and tasks.

There's a greater likelihood that you will complete all of the tasks you set for yourself if you know exactly what you need to get done each day. You see, in a busy, stressful workday, being aware of what has to be done and setting aside some time to dedicate your energies to your chores can sometimes make all the difference.

2. Never omit lunch.

Don't miss dinner or breakfast either. To perform well, eat well. Consume nutritious foods throughout your break to refuel after working in the operations research room or the accounting office. Make sure you eat healthily since if you don't; you may find it difficult to concentrate on your task or fall asleep. If you stop to consider it, the few minutes you spend dozing off and letting your thoughts wander might easily mount up to an hour or two. Additionally, you'll be working considerably more slowly, which will reduce your efficiency. The main conclusion is that your brain and stomach can only work together, so eat when it's time to eat.

3. If you truly need to do a challenging assignment in a few hours, don't be scared to put a "Do Not Disturb" sign on your office door.

Professionals must help coworkers realize when it is acceptable to stop by for a quick conversation and when it is not appropriate to bring in outside distractions, just as kids must learn how to say "no." You'll definitely want to do this more frequently if you find that having your workplace to yourself for a few hours increases productivity, particularly if your duties need a lot of time and effort to complete.

4. Make sure everything is well-organized!

Make your desk clear. Keep essential documents apart from scratch paper. Maintain a record of your appointments, deadlines, and calendar. Do not use the last desk drawer as a garbage can, and keep your coffee mug away from official contracts. Make room for yourself so that your mind is free. Unless you are among those who thrive in disorganized workspaces, tidy up after yourself and maintain a clean environment. You'll save many minutes of searching for keys, organizing emergency files, and other tasks by doing this.

Make sure everything in your office is accurately accounted for. Assign folders or file holders to related tasks and dispose of waste in the appropriate location. Purchase inexpensive pen holders and other desk organizers to help you keep everything you need for work visible without taking up too much space on your desk.

5. Acquire the skill of leaving when you run out of options. Then, return when you're prepared or when you've finished all of your other responsibilities.

You have to learn to put down the paper if you've been staring at it for more than an hour, your creative juices aren't working, or you're just having a bad day. If you force yourself to think of something, you'll just be wasting more time, so go on. Walk away now since there are more important things to attend to, and finishing them early will allow you more time to return to that unachievable project proposal or uninteresting pitch. Sometimes, you just need to walk away in order to regain control of your time and stress level.

Efficiency

Efficiency is the capacity to complete tasks swiftly and successfully while wasting as little time, energy, or effort as possible. It is an essential component of time management since it enables you to work more efficiently and accomplish your objectives. Here are some pointers for increasing time management effectiveness:

1. Establish reasonable goals: Achieving efficiency in time management requires setting reasonable goals. Prioritize your goals based on whether they can be completed in the allotted time.

2. Concentrate on one task at a time: Multitasking can be inefficient and result in time and energy loss. You may accomplish a

task more quickly and effectively if you concentrate on it one at a time. Prioritize your work and keep distractions at bay to make sure you are concentrating on the things that matter most.

3. Make use of automation and technology: Technology may be a very effective tool for increasing time management productivity. To automate repetitive operations and optimize workflow, use automation solutions like task management software. Make use of productivity tools, such as time-tracking applications, to monitor your progress and keep on course.

4. Develop delegation skills: Assigning responsibilities to others can help you manage your time more effectively. Determine which duties can be assigned to others, then assign

them to people who possess the required knowledge and experience. This enables you to concentrate on things that need more of your attention and are more vital.

5. Set task priorities: Increasing time management efficiency requires setting task priorities. This enables you to concentrate on the most crucial tasks and accomplish your objectives more quickly.

6. Avoid procrastination: One of the biggest barriers to effective time management is procrastination. Assign due dates to assignments and honour them. Divide complicated jobs into smaller, more doable ones, and then take each one on one at a time. You'll be able to stay motivated and save time by doing this.

7. Take breaks: Improving time management efficiency requires taking breaks. You can reenergize and refocus, which increases your effectiveness and productivity. Make sure you plan regular pause times during the day so that you can recuperate, unwind, and rejuvenate.

To sum up, effectiveness is a vital component of time management. You may increase your productivity and accomplish your goals more successfully by prioritizing work, learning to delegate, utilizing technology and automation, focusing on one task at a time, setting reasonable goals, taking breaks, and not procrastinating.

To make sure your tactics still align with your current priorities and objectives, don't forget to examine and tweak them on a frequent basis.

We'll talk about overcoming procrastination and maintaining motivation in the next part.

d. Occasionally, answers can be found outside of the field you are investigating.

The princes in the tale paid attention to everyone, including fish, insects, and small children. The best ideas might occasionally emerge from unexpected places. This makes me think of the legend surrounding the first outdoor glass lift in history. The narrative proceeds as follows:

The El Cortez Hotel, formerly the focal point of San Diego's downtown, was having issues with its lone lift. They intended to add lift. After much deliberation, they agreed to tear down the hotel for a few months, drill holes in the ceilings and begin construction on the lift. The hotel caretaker overheard the engineers at the hotel having their last conversations about how they were going to carry out the work.

"Are you going to close down the hotel to build the lift?" he asked them as he walked up to them.

The engineers gave a mocking nod.

"Why, that will result in a loss of revenue to the management and impact the livelihood of people like me," the caretaker questioned.

"Do you have any alternate suggestion?" the engineers inquired.

After giving it some thought, the caretaker said, "Why don't you build the lift outside the hotel and connect it?"

The engineers rejected the notion at first, but with time, they began to realize that it did make sense. Thus, the El Cortez Hotel erected the first exterior glass lift in history in the early 1950s. Heralded as the world's first of its kind, the Ilikai in Waikiki, Hawaii, and the Fairmont in San Francisco later adopted its design. The views of the city from the El Cortez lift were astounding.

Thus, pay attention to what everyone has to say and emphasize audialterampartem in accordance with one of the three natural justice principles. "Hear the other side" or "hear both sides" is what the maxim refers to. To put it another way, the party who stands to lose out from the authority's judgement must be given a hearing.

e. Nuisances can be the source of problems.

The princes had no idea that one of their fish would not dry up because of a little ant attacking a small child. Because the world is a complicated network of relationships, it can occasionally be very challenging to comprehend cause and effect.

For example, it is possible that your employer became enraged with you during the meeting because of an altercation he had with his wife earlier in the day. Alternatively, your subordinate may have been experiencing severe financial difficulties, which has led to his poor performance and negatively impacted your team.

I'm not arguing that we can fix every person's difficulties. The key takeaway is that there may be valid causes for a person's unexpected actions or abrupt reactions. When things calm down, it is always a good idea to stand back, watch, and inquire as to why. It is advised to consider things from another person's point of view and put yourself in their position. Being a good leader requires empathy. It is appropriate to chastise underachievers, but only after understanding their motivations.

f. Diminish your ego

The princes mixed with everyone and showed no conceit about their regal status. They were able to identify the true cause because of this. They would never have discovered the true reason if they had fired the farmer or the cow for using excuses that appeared to transfer the blame. An organization's progress is hampered greatly by ego. Keep in mind that remaining detached is not the same as ego.

It is important to support individuals in an organization or in partnerships to openly share their opinions. Problems can only be effectively solved at that point. Naturally, there will always be a grumpy person who needs to be dealt with gently or tactfully. Overconfidence produces walls and unfounded worries that obstruct the free exchange of knowledge and ultimately cause a vortex to collapse. Allow me to tell you a little story to illustrate how the ego can cause blindness.

The only thing that could have bridged the abyss was the trunk of a fallen tree, and even then, two squirrels could not have passed each other safely. Even the most courageous would have shuddered at the tight road, but not our goats. But neither could put aside their pride to support the other.

A goat stepped onto the log. The other followed suit. They met horn to horn in the middle. They each plunged into the raging torrent below, unable to give way to the other.

Step 7: Hiring Helpers

While breaking harmful habits is never simple, it can be made a lot simpler with the help of friends and family. The people in your life have the power to offer responsibility and support, both of which are crucial while attempting to break a habit. As you take on this endeavour, get in touch with them if you need assistance or even just some moral support.

Locating a group of like-minded people who share your goals on the internet can also be helpful. This can help you feel friendship and serve as a reminder that you're not travelling alone.

Making connections with people who are aware of your struggles can be quite beneficial for maintaining motivation and focus.

Tell your loved ones about your objectives and solicit their assistance. They are able to support you and hold you responsible.

Additionally, think about consulting with a time management or ADHD-focused coach or therapist. They may offer you tailored guidance and assist you in developing efficient time management techniques.

Joining an online forum or support group with others who face comparable difficulties could also be beneficial. It can be immensely empowering to connect with those who have similar struggles with tardiness behaviours. It can be quite beneficial to have a confidant with whom to share tales, discuss, and receive advice.

Whatever you do, keep in mind that it's a process that calls for perseverance and commitment. It takes time to break the habit of being late, but if you have the correct support system and methods in place, you can succeed! Wishing you luck!

Bonus Step 8: Monitor Your Development and Honour Victories

Lastly, remember to acknowledge and enjoy your accomplishments! Reward yourself for your achievements when you begin to make progress towards your goals. Honouring minor victories keeps you inspired and reaffirms that your efforts have been worthwhile.

Determine the benchmarks or incentives that will keep you on course. This could be as easy as giving yourself a nice treat after finishing a task on schedule. Or even a day off whenever you accomplish a particular degree of achievement. Maintaining a progress log and acknowledging your accomplishments will help you stay motivated and focused.

Workspace Decluttering Exercises

It's common knowledge that an untidy workstation will naturally reduce productivity. But, the messiness alone can lead to unneeded stress and overload. Getting your surroundings organized is a process that takes time to complete. Have patience with yourself and resolve to gradually implement tiny, regular improvements. Your productivity and time-management abilities will increase as a result, and you'll be more capable of handling even the most difficult jobs.

The following are some practical suggestions for organizing your workstation and increasing output:

Efficiency is the capacity to complete tasks swiftly and successfully while wasting as little time, energy, or effort as possible. It is an essential component of time management since it enables you to work more efficiently and accomplish your objectives. Here are some pointers for increasing time management effectiveness:

1. Establish reasonable goals: Achieving efficiency in time management requires setting reasonable goals. Prioritize your goals based on whether they can be completed in the allotted time.

2. Concentrate on one task at a time: Multitasking can be inefficient and result in time and energy loss. You may accomplish a task more quickly and effectively if you concentrate on it one at a time. Prioritize your

work and keep distractions at bay to make sure you are concentrating on the things that matter most.

3. Make use of automation and technology: Technology may be a very effective tool for increasing time management productivity. To automate repetitive operations and optimize workflow, use automation solutions like task management software. Make use of productivity tools, such as time-tracking applications, to monitor your progress and keep on course.

4. Develop delegation skills: Assigning responsibilities to others can help you manage your time more effectively. Determine which duties can be assigned to others, then assign them to people who possess the required knowledge and experience. This enables you to

concentrate on things that need more of your attention and are more vital.

5. Set task priorities: Increasing time management efficiency requires setting task priorities. This enables you to concentrate on the most crucial tasks and accomplish your objectives more quickly.

6. Avoid procrastination: One of the biggest barriers to effective time management is procrastination. Assign due dates to assignments and honour them. Divide complicated jobs into smaller, more doable ones, and then take each one on one at a time. You'll be able to stay motivated and save time by doing this.

7. Take breaks: Improving time management efficiency requires taking breaks. You can reenergize and refocus, which increases your

effectiveness and productivity. Make sure you plan regular pause times during the day so that you can recuperate, unwind, and rejuvenate.

To sum up, effectiveness is a vital component of time management. You may increase your productivity and accomplish your goals more successfully by prioritizing work, learning to delegate, utilizing technology and automation, focusing on one task at a time, setting reasonable goals, taking breaks, and not procrastinating.

To make sure your tactics still align with your current priorities and objectives, don't forget to examine and tweak them on a frequent basis.

We'll talk about overcoming procrastination and maintaining motivation in the next part.
d. Occasionally, answers can be found outside of the field you are investigating.

The princes in the tale paid attention to everyone, including fish, insects, and small children. The best ideas might occasionally emerge from unexpected places. This makes me think of the legend surrounding the first outdoor glass lift in history. The narrative proceeds as follows:

The El Cortez Hotel, formerly the focal point of San Diego's downtown, was having issues with its lone lift. They intended to add lift. After much deliberation, they agreed to tear down the hotel for a few months, drill holes in the ceilings and begin construction on the lift. The hotel caretaker overheard the engineers at the hotel having their last conversations about how they were going to carry out the work.

"Are you going to close down the hotel to build the lift?" he asked them as he walked up to them.

The engineers gave a mocking nod.

"Why, that will result in a loss of revenue to the management and impact the livelihood of people like me," the caretaker questioned.

"Do you have any alternate suggestion?" the engineers inquired.

After giving it some thought, the caretaker said, "Why don't you build the lift outside the hotel and connect it?"

The engineers rejected the notion at first, but with time, they began to realize that it did make sense. Thus, the El Cortez Hotel erected the first exterior glass lift in history in the early 1950s. Heralded as the world's first of its kind, the Ilikai in Waikiki, Hawaii, and the Fairmont in San Francisco later adopted its design. The views of the city from the El Cortez lift were astounding.

Thus, pay attention to what everyone has to say and emphasize audialterampartem in accordance with one of the three natural justice principles. "Hear the other side" or "hear both sides" is what the maxim refers to. To put it another way, the party who stands to lose out from the authority's judgement must be given a hearing.

e. Nuisances can be the source of problems.

The princes had no idea that one of their fish would not dry up because of a little ant attacking a small child. Because the world is a complicated network of relationships, it can occasionally be very challenging to comprehend cause and effect.

For example, it is possible that your employer became enraged with you during the meeting because of an altercation he had with his wife earlier in the day. Alternatively, your subordinate may have been experiencing severe financial difficulties, which has led to his poor performance and negatively impacted your team.

I'm not arguing that we can fix every person's difficulties. The key takeaway is that there may be valid causes for a person's unexpected actions or abrupt reactions. When things calm down, it is always a good idea to stand back, watch, and inquire as to why. It is advised to consider things from another person's point of view and put yourself in their position. Being a good leader requires empathy. It is appropriate to chastise underachievers, but only after understanding their motivations.

f. Diminish your ego

The princes mixed with everyone and showed no conceit about their regal status. They were able to identify the true cause because of this. They would never have discovered the true reason if they had fired the farmer or the cow for using excuses that appeared to transfer the blame. An organization's progress is hampered greatly by ego. Keep in mind that remaining detached is not the same as ego.

It is important to support individuals in an organization or in partnerships to openly share their opinions. Problems can only be effectively solved at that point. Naturally, there will always be a grumpy person who needs to be dealt with gently or tactfully. Overconfidence produces walls and unfounded worries that obstruct the free exchange of knowledge and ultimately cause a vortex to collapse. Allow me to tell you a little story to illustrate how the ego can cause blindness.

The only thing that could have bridged the abyss was the trunk of a fallen tree, and even then, two squirrels could not have passed each other safely. Even the most courageous would have shuddered at the tight road, but not our goats. But neither could put aside their pride to support the other.

A goat stepped onto the log. The other followed suit. They met horn to horn in the middle. They each plunged into the raging torrent below, unable to give way to the other.

Step 7: Hiring Helpers

While breaking harmful habits is never simple, it can be made a lot simpler with the help of friends and family. The people in your life have the power to offer responsibility and support, both of which are crucial while attempting to break a habit. As you take on this endeavour, get in touch with them if you need assistance or even just some moral support.

Locating a group of like-minded people who share your goals on the internet can also be helpful. This can help you feel friendship and serve as a reminder that you're not travelling alone.

Making connections with people who are aware of your struggles can be quite beneficial for maintaining motivation and focus.

Tell your loved ones about your objectives and solicit their assistance. They are able to support you and hold you responsible.

Additionally, think about consulting with a time management or ADHD-focused coach or therapist. They may offer you tailored guidance and assist you in developing efficient time management techniques.

Joining an online forum or support group with others who face comparable difficulties could also be beneficial. It can be immensely empowering to connect with those who have similar struggles with tardiness behaviours. It can be quite beneficial to have a confidant with whom to share tales, discuss, and receive advice.

Whatever you do, keep in mind that it's a process that calls for perseverance and commitment. It takes time to break the habit of being late, but if you have the correct support system and methods in place, you can succeed! Wishing you luck!

Bonus Step 8: Monitor Your Development and Honour Victories

Lastly, remember to acknowledge and enjoy your accomplishments! Reward yourself for your achievements when you begin to make progress towards your goals. Honouring minor victories keeps you inspired and reaffirms that your efforts have been worthwhile.

Determine the benchmarks or incentives that will keep you on course. This could be as easy as giving yourself a nice treat after finishing a task on schedule. Or even a day off whenever you accomplish a particular degree of achievement. Maintaining a progress log and acknowledging your accomplishments will help you stay motivated and focused.

Workspace Decluttering Exercises

It's common knowledge that an untidy workstation will naturally reduce productivity. But, the messiness alone can lead to unneeded stress and overload. Getting your surroundings organized is a process that takes time to complete. Have patience with yourself and resolve to gradually implement tiny, regular improvements. Your productivity and time-management abilities will increase as a result, and you'll be more capable of handling even the most difficult jobs.

The following are some practical suggestions for organizing your workstation and increasing output:

1. Plan Your Breaks: Plan your breaks in the same way that you plan your tasks. Consider these meetings with yourself as non-negotiable appointments. Additionally, this can assist in

letting people know that you are inaccessible during these hours.

2. Take Breaks Away from Your Workspace: Try to avoid spending breaks in front of your desk. This can facilitate the establishment of a defined boundary between work and break times.

3. Take Part in Non-Working Activities During Breaks: Make use of your break time to partake in non-work related activities. This can aid in mental relaxation and help one break away from work-related thinking.

4. Exercise Mindfulness: Make use of your breaks to engage in mindful exercises. This could be as simple as sitting quietly or practising mindful eating and deep breathing. It has been demonstrated that mindfulness increases focus and lowers stress.

5. Steer Clear of Digital Devices: Try to stay away from digital devices during breaks.

Staying connected all the time can make it hard to turn off the job and truly unwind.

To sum up, taking regular breaks is crucial to preserving concentration, averting burnout, and improving general job performance. Working smarter, not harder, is the goal. Recall that productivity is determined by the calibre of the job completed during a given period as well as the amount of time spent working. Taking regular breaks can greatly enhance that quality, producing better outcomes and promoting a more positive work-life balance.

The Significance Of Proficient Time Management.

•It could help in meeting deadlines

Not only are deadlines and appointments difficult to remember but they can easily be overlooked if one is not careful.

An organisation that barely reaches its goals may find that effective time management is crucial. Keeping all of your appointments and due dates in one place facilitates more effective time management.

Effective time management has the potential to improve focus and productivity.

Learning how to manage your time effectively and knowing when and how to focus your efforts are key components of time management, which goes well beyond just adding more tasks to your list. As a result, the majority of business owners will see an increase in production and an improvement in the efficiency of their company, which is always advantageous.

- Less procrastination may result from better time management.

Likewise, most will discover that implementing better time management practices at work will often help to lessen procrastination. You'll be less distracted, and everyone will be able to finish the job sooner if you and your team are more focused on the current task.

It will be simpler for you to concentrate when you are working under a set schedule with duties assigned to particular time slots throughout the day. This is because you will be aware that each task has a deadline that you must meet.

Consequently, you won't put off working on such duties as much. As a result, you'll acquire more effective procrastination management skills.

- A well-planned schedule can result in greater freedom and less stress.

It's stressful to race against the clock to meet a deadline since you never know if you'll succeed. However, having good time management skills enables you to view your workday as a series of tasks that you must complete rather than as a whole.

It is simple to prioritise your tasks and establish plans that will ensure you don't experience too much stress once you have all of your responsibilities organised and know exactly when you will need to complete each one.

Others might be surprised to learn that managing your time will often be much more liberating and reduce stress at work. You'll frequently be able to achieve a better work-life balance when you set out time for specific tasks or projects and are aware of what has to be accomplished.

- It maintains your standing in the workplace.

If you give lousy time management enough time, it will definitely damage your reputation. Other obvious consequences of poor time management include missing deadlines, rushing assignments, and skipping meetings.

Effective time management, however, eliminates these chances and aids in building and maintaining your professional reputation.

- It also helps avoid expensive fines.

Your business involves more than just meeting project deadlines; for instance, you must ensure that taxes are paid on schedule. Unless, of course, you wish to pay an additional 5% fee for each month that your return is late.

You'll stay out of trouble if you set up a specific period on your calendar for handling taxes and other expenses in your business.

- Effective time management could help achieve a better work-life balance.

When you manage your time well, you will create a formal schedule for your days.

Additionally, you'll be well on your way to creating a clear work-life balance when you track how your day is divided between professional and personal responsibilities. one that guarantees you'll have time for both.

Fear: A formidable enemy

Your minds were created with our safety in mind. Not only in terms of body but also mentally. Your brain will make every effort to keep you out of awkward situations. It acts in this way on autopilot due to its survival impulses. Recognise that your brain is attempting to shield you from fears that are different from what they used to be.

I would never have accomplished anything in life if I had paid attention to their anxieties. Since many of you may not be able to relate, allow me to clarify how fear and productivity are related. According to a recent study on physiology, most of the motivation for any work we wish to perform comes from fear. Examples of such fears include dread of failing exams, worry of running out of money, fear of losing your current job, and a host of other fears.

We are afraid of the unknown. We are afraid of things we do not know. Something becomes less scary the more you do it. When you reflect on your life, the times you have overcome your anxieties and discovered the most about yourself are usually the ones when you have had to face your fears.

It is impossible to get rid of all of your fears. And it's acceptable. It's just the sensation of fear that makes things uncomfortable, but with experience and confronting increasing amounts of anxiety, one can learn to manage this sensation.

Eleanor Roosevelt once said, "Do one thing that scares you every day."

dread, no matter how tiny or large, will change dramatically if you take action. Rather than being an uncomfortable feeling, dread will serve as a motivator to increase your output.

Being Rely on Inspiration and Motivation
Inspiration and motivation by themselves are worthless. Don't rely on inspiration and motivation to help you reach your goals; they will ultimately fall short if you want to accomplish anything. Had I simply worked when I was inspired, I never would have progressed, and it might have taken me an additional two or three years to finish this book instead of just four months. Putting a structure in place is essential to completing tasks.

Starting is the most difficult aspect. It is a mechanism, much like the action plan we will soon discover, that will enable you to persevere even in the face of motivation. Additionally, once you understand that resistance is common and a necessary component of the process and that inspiration and motivation are merely fleeting emotions that will pass, you may begin working on a solution. To reverse this, here is a fantastic quotation about what separates amateurs from experts that I really adore.

An amateur waits for a spark of inspiration. The others simply get up and head to work.

This quote emphasises something very basic. Creativity is absurd. What matters most is to actually sit down and get started.

Seek out more useful guidance and recommendations as opposed to motivating and inspirational ones. Because they are immediately usable and will always be available for you, practically every chapter in this book focuses on practical tools, strategies, and a system. Encouragement, beliefs, useful counsel, and a system work wonders.

Another aspect of motivation is that it is ephemeral and not something you can depend on indefinitely. You might be motivated to do a task today, but eventually, that enthusiasm will wear off, and you won't be able to work on it at all.

Making Use of Dead Time

Dead time is the time you spend waiting in a queue, on a bus, on a train, in a car, etc. You will frequently have to wait for things to happen. How do you handle situations such as these? Just wait, sleep, play on your phone or video game, watch a YouTube video, browse through your Instagram and Facebook feed, or play a video game. For many, it is like this. Why not be productive with this time instead?

Make the most of your idle time by taking notes, studying, researching, finishing tasks, reading, reviewing your schedule, or catching up with friends and family. Do you know how much you can accomplish and how much you might be doing during that forty-minute bus or vehicle ride? All the time if you total it up. You may use all that time to develop your projects, business, and career. Why not give an audiobook or podcast episode about a topic that will make your life better a listen? Take-out drives are ideal times to do some serious creativity. The voice recorder on your phone makes it simple to record yourself. Once you're back home, you can listen back over your recording and jot down any notes.

Additionally, you can meditate to learn more about your life and existence. Yes, you read correctly—meditation doesn't require a certain posture; you can practise it while seated on a chair or even in a car. In the last chapter, I'll go into more detail on how meditation might increase productivity.

Now, you could come across a few worthwhile podcasts and audiobooks that you might find interesting. Once more, it's not that you can't browse Facebook—of course you can. Just keep in mind that if you're following this book, you'll probably be going after anything by then.

Therefore, manage your time well and make the most of it. Utilise that time to enhance your life's quality.

Respecting the demands and schedules of other people is the true essence of being punctual.

Respecting the demands and schedules of other people is the true essence of being punctual. It's a sign that you value other people's time, and since you won't have to worry about being late, you'll probably feel less worried. Since we are all aware of how unpleasant it is when someone is late for an appointment, why inflict that feeling on others?

It also helps to think of ourselves as members of a team or group, and our responsibility to arrive on time is reflected in that group. Everyone in that group or team will lose credibility and respect if they are perpetually late.

Money is time.

Money is time. Additionally, you lose time that you could be using to work and get money if you are late. It's crucial to arrive on time because of this. Being on time demonstrates your regard for your company, colleagues, and clients, who will value your self-control in being there on time.

- AIM TO BE ON TIME FOR ALL ACTIVITIES THAT DEMAND ON TIME (E.G., MEETINGS, APPOINTMENTS).

ASK THE PERSON HOSTING THEM TO CHECK IN WITH YOU (OR SEND AN EMAIL) PRIOR TO EVERYONE ELSE ARRIVING; THIS SHOWS RESPECT FOR THEIR TIME AS WELL! ARRIVE 5 TO 15 MINUTES EARLY FOR MEETINGS OR APPOINTMENTS!

In what way does power relate to punctuality?

Being on time is a sign of strength. People will notice your strong work ethic and consideration for others if you are the one who consistently arrives on time. By showcasing your effective time management skills, you are gaining people's trust and taking on greater responsibilities.

Additionally, managers or supervisors must arrive on time since it demonstrates to their staff that they value them as persons. "My boss cares enough about me that he/she wants us all here early on Monday morning so we can get started right away," a worker could believe.

Being punctual demonstrates your respect for other people's time and effort.

One of the best ways to respect people is to arrive on time. It shows that you don't value their time when you arrive late. Your timetable may take precedence over theirs if you're late all the time. Being on time demonstrates your respect for their time and preferences, as well as your want to keep the relationship going.

Would productivity in your office decrease if everyone arrived at work ten minutes early or more? Most likely not; you would simply adjust by shaving off time in between appointments and getting dressed early. Because of this, both parties can gain by being on time: It reduces stress for all parties involved, including yourself, by keeping things flowing well for everyone.

Being on time also helps others because when they are waiting on someone else who is running late, all they can think about is how much they detest being kept waiting! While it may seem obvious to avoid making other people wait needlessly, at Punctuality Headquarters, we'll be honest and say that occasionally, even those of us who place the highest value on our punctual habits can become entangled in our drama.

Being on time demonstrates professionalism, which might advance your work.

One of the most crucial things to keep in mind in business is punctuality, particularly when it comes to arriving on time for appointments and meetings. Arriving late can lead to numerous issues and give you a bad impression in the eyes of your supervisor, clients, and colleagues. If you're late for everything, people can assume you're not reliable for certain jobs. Given how long it takes you to get to work on time every morning, they may be afraid that if they give you their deadlines, you won't meet them.

Even if someone is only five minutes late for everything they do every day, it still demonstrates how unorganised and careless they are. That person doesn't care about meeting deadlines or expectations, so he won't get anything done on time. Instead, he puts his own needs first. He doesn't want others to put pressure on him to do something other than what he wants to do at the moment, which could cause him to stray from finishing his current tasks or personal projects because those other things now take precedence over completing whatever was put in front of him (which means no one wins).

How to Become a Better Time Manager

By developing your time management abilities, you will become a more productive worker and a more competitive applicant when you apply for new chances. The following advice will help you become more skilled at time management:

1. Specify your short- and long-term goals.

Setting goals on a regular basis may help you fully comprehend what it takes to attain specific results. To assist you in achieving more ambitious, long-term goals, consider setting smaller checkpoints along the journey. If your objective is to advance within the next six months, you may need to make smaller goals to focus on developing specific talents. Your objectives must be precise, quantifiable, reasonable, timely, and pertinent.

2. Monitor your schedule.

Setting aside time to do the most crucial tasks on your list is a necessary part of time management. Consider routinely marking off particular time slots on your calendar so that you have time for yourself without distractions or meetings. It is advisable to contemplate if it is beneficial for you to participate in specific gatherings. If you don't think you'll be able to offer anything of value or participate at all, you should be free to turn down invitations to certain gatherings. Think things out and proceed with caution if you decide to do this. To clarify your choice, you might wish to consider emailing the meeting's owner.

3. Sort your jobs according to priority.

Setting priorities is a tough discipline to master, but it becomes simpler with experience. Making to-do lists can help you practice prioritisation. If you make a list of everything you need to do and put it on paper or your computer, you can physically prioritise the chores that are most important or simple. Ask your manager or a coworker who is great at setting priorities how they would finish a task if you need assistance. If you understand deadlines, how a task affects other people and company objectives, you may be able to finish projects sooner than others. If you are still unable to finish the assignment by the deadline, you may be eligible to request an extension of the deadline.

By improving your time management abilities, you may work more efficiently and comprehensively throughout the day. You may improve your time management skills by setting priorities for your to-do list, being organised, and setting goals.

Say "yes" when you want to say "no" sometimes.

One way to improve your time management at work is to learn when to say no to requests. It could be tough to finish your work on time if you accept non-priority work, for example, if you're trying to meet a deadline. If you have a tight deadline and can't help with a project, your colleagues will understand.

5. Don't put things off.

Setting priorities and procrastinating are two different things. Make sure nothing gets completely crossed off the list when prioritising your chores. It's acceptable to put off less crucial tasks until another day. When assignments are routinely pushed off for the day, it's called procrastination.

Page 5: Time Management Solutions for Teams: To make sure everyone is in agreement and deadlines are reached effectively if you work in a team, take into consideration utilising collaborative time management solutions like shared calendars, project management software, and communication platforms.

The Time Management Power of Saying "No": It's a useful skill to learn how to say "no" to assignments, obligations, or initiatives that don't fit your priorities or ambitions. You can safeguard your time and concentrate on the things that really count.

The Matrix of Time-Blocking: Make a matrix where your jobs are categorised according to priority and urgency. This can assist you in making efficient use of your time and preventing yourself from becoming mired down in unimportant duties.

Energy Levels and Time Management: Throughout the day, be aware of your natural energy levels. Plan mentally taxing and high-priority chores for when you are at your most energetic; use your low-energy periods for less taxing work.

Time Management for Complicated Projects: Divide big, complicated projects into smaller, more doable jobs. Track progress and dependencies by using project management tools like Gantt charts and Kanban boards.

Time Management for Procrastination: To get past your first reluctance to begin a task, use strategies like the "Two-Minute Rule" if you suffer from procrastination. Once you get going, you frequently gain momentum.

Developing Time Management and Delegation Skills: Invest time in team members' training and mentorship to help them become more skilled. This may eventually lessen the necessity for your direct participation in specific tasks.

Time Management for Personal Development: Set aside time for education and personal growth. Continuous learning can improve your abilities and efficacy, whether it is through reading, taking classes, or going to seminars.

Managing Time During Emergencies: Utilise time and resource management techniques such as the Emergency Operations Centre (EOC) frameworks or the Incident Command

System (ICS) in high-stress or emergency scenarios.

Time management for business owners: Business owners frequently have a wide variety of duties. Give jobs that have a direct bearing on company growth priority, and whenever possible, automate or outsource repetitive work.

Students can gain from time management strategies such as the "Pomodoro Technique" and making thorough study plans. It takes precise time management to juggle extracurricular activities, part-time work, and academics.

Setting limits and managing your time: Define distinct boundaries between your personal and professional lives. This promotes a good work-life balance and lessens the risk of burnout.

Time Management for Creatives: Setting aside specific time for creativity, brainstorming, and creative exploration can be beneficial for creatives. This period needs to be preserved for creative thought.

Time management with Mind Mapping: To graphically arrange your ideas and duties, apply mind mapping techniques. This may help you see your priorities and objectives more clearly.

Constant Evaluation and Adjustment: Evaluate your time management techniques on a regular basis and be willing to make changes. Your strategy ought to adjust when your obligations, objectives, and situation do.

The "One Thing" Principle with Time Management: Decide which task is the most crucial of the day and give it top priority. Getting this work done might provide you with direction and a sense of accomplishment.

The Method of "Two-List": Keep two different to-do lists: one for everyday tasks and another for projects and long-term objectives. You can better balance your long-term goals and urgent requirements with this.

Flexibility Vs. Productivity

In the ever-evolving landscape of work, two fundamental concepts often find themselves at odds: flexibility and productivity. The pursuit of greater flexibility in the workplace, characterized by remote work arrangements, flexible schedules, and reduced rigidity, can sometimes appear to clash with the relentless pursuit of productivity, efficiency, and performance. In this exploration, we'll delve into the dynamics between flexibility and productivity, examining how they intersect, the challenges they pose, and the strategies to strike a harmonious balance.

Defining Flexibility

Flexibility in the workplace refers to the freedom employees have to shape their work environment, schedules, and methods to suit their needs. It encompasses various elements:

Remote Work: The ability to work from locations outside the traditional office, often facilitated by digital technologies.

Flexible Hours: The option to set one's work hours, accommodating personal preferences and responsibilities.

Autonomy: The freedom to make decisions about how tasks are completed, fostering a sense of ownership and empowerment.

The Importance of Flexibility

Enhanced Job Satisfaction: The autonomy and freedom that flexibility provides can increase job satisfaction and motivation.

Diverse Talent Pool: Organizations can access a broader range of talent by accommodating individuals who may have difficulty with traditional work arrangements.

Defining Productivity

Productivity, on the other hand, is the measure of how efficiently resources—especially time and effort—are converted into desired outcomes. In the workplace, it typically refers to achieving more significant results in less time.

The Drive for Productivity

Productivity is highly valued for several reasons:

Economic Competitiveness: Productivity contributes to economic growth and competitiveness on both individual and organizational levels.

Efficiency: Productive work environments streamline processes, reduce waste, and ensure optimal resource utilization.

Performance: High productivity can lead to increased profitability, which is essential for the sustainability and success of businesses.

Giving Feedback

Letting it slide is the worst thing that you can do!

Avoiding tough conversations is not taking the high road, nor is it the kind of thing to do. Have you ever seen a colleague struggling with bad behaviour and being left alone? You might have done that because you didn't want to ruffle any feathers. This is not the way to lead from your highest self's core values.

Let's reframe discomfort in tough conversations as generative tension.

Some tough, brave conversations that are necessary to be had, like tough performance feedback or bias interruption, WILL feel uncomfortable in your body. Let's reframe that discomfort as generative tension, a necessary feeling we must feel to get to a greater good and be in alignment with our values.

TAKE ACTION

Brene Brown has created a brilliant Engaged Feedback Checklist that you can download and review before giving tough feedback.

When giving feedback, you want to ask permission to give feedback, focus on the impact of the behaviour/pattern of behaviour vs their character, name your feelings modelling a willingness to be open, ask how you want to engage differently in the future and check in on how the feedback is sitting with the person.

Jot down your talking points beforehand if that is helpful to you. The goal here is to have a clear and complete conversation about this troublesome pattern or experience, being sure to express the impact of the behaviour.

For example, "When X happens, I feel Y because ___. I imagine you intended to ___. What might work better for me in the future is _____. How does this feedback resonate with you?" Plan to say this aloud in a role-play practice with your partner, stuffed animal, or dog if that helps.

REMEMBER: Never give other people tough feedback on their behalf. This might feel like you're doing them a favour, but really, you're denying your colleagues the opportunity to grow as leaders.

To be a manager who gives feedback routinely, it's critical to assess your progress with this. Set milestones to hold yourself accountable. Get an accountability partner. Routinely giving feedback to your direct reports from a place of continuous positive regard for your colleagues can be beneficial. You may find that this extra social support and nudge from peers was the missing link you've been seeking. You must broach the conversation with your team around creating a goal to do this as a team, creating milestones, and even celebrating progress as you hit some of these milestones.

You can't expect a 1-litre soda from a shot glass.

Remember that everyone is operating from the level of consciousness that they're at. Try to meet that reality with empathy rather than frustration. Therefore, while not excusing bad behaviour, it's important to understand that it's also unkind and unrealistic to expect anything from anyone unable or unwilling to do that, even when it's the right thing to do. You may have direct reports who may be unwilling or unable to receive constructive feedback.

TAKE ACTION

Write a journal around the following prompt: "What would it look and feel like to match your expectations of others to the truth of what they have to offer with no judgment?"

The Toxic High Performer

The highly productive, efficient, yet toxic direct report often gets little or no feedback. We tend to excuse their bad behaviour because they are so productive. "They just know how to get stuff done" is the common excuse I hear when conversations emerge around what to do with the toxic high performer on your team. To really tackle this, you first have to debunk the notion that high performance is just about outcomes. The means matter just as much as the ends. You have to find out whether or not this person is coachable. Some people are truly unaware of how people experience them, and once that is brought to their attention, they can change. If they're not coachable and you've done everything you can do to coach them, then you want to help them transition with dignity to a different role or company.

Tough conversations with Senior Managers or Peers

Some of the tough conversations you'll have maybe with your manager. You must be forthright with sharing ideas and feedback without being overly concerned about how things will be received.

For example, career pathways in so many companies are unclear at best and inequitable at worst. In most companies, you can't take a back seat and expect to effortlessly be upwardly mobile. If you've ever found yourself wondering, I'm already doing the work of a more senior manager. Why is no one promoting me?

They posted a job description to hire for a role I'm perfectly suited for. Why wouldn't they just promote me?

It's time for you to have a conversation with key decision-makers who can influence that decision, including your manager and others with decision-making power. You want to talk about your role, noting your:

Demonstrated capabilities to date.

Vision for what you could do in the role you desire.

Process and timeline for how you'll be evaluated for this role.

If you already know you'll be promoted, take the following steps below.

Understanding Your Priorities

Understanding your priorities is an essential aspect of effective time management.

To understand your priorities, it is important to start by setting clear goals for yourself. Once you have identified your goals, you can then prioritize your tasks and activities based on how they align with your goals.

Tasks are divided into four categories:

Urgent and important tasks

Important but not urgent tasks

Urgent but not important tasks

Neither urgent nor important tasks

Another key aspect of understanding your priorities is learning to say no. When we try to take on too many tasks or commitments, we can become overwhelmed and lose focus on our most important goals.

In conclusion, understanding your priorities is a critical aspect of effective time management. By setting clear goals, using tools like the Eisenhower Matrix, and learning to say no to tasks and commitments that do not align with our priorities, we can maximize our productivity and achieve our goals more efficiently.

Identifying Personal Time Management Challenges

We'll inevitably face a few roadblocks when trying to become better versions of ourselves. Many people cite a lack of time as the reason they don't fulfil their dreams. And ironically, they often refuse to look back at how they've spent the time they had. By following along, you should be free from this issue. Take a moment to acknowledge and celebrate this, but be mindful. There are other obstacles you are likely to face, some of which are specific to your surroundings, so let's examine some of the more common hardships we may face in adopting Time Management.

Another frequent difficulty is trying to take on too many things. Having looked at it all the time, it's easy to scribble down dozens of ideas we would like to do every day. But there's a key problem here. In Alec Mackenzie's The Time Trap, he rightly points out a lack of priorities as the source of this struggle. He says, "Without goals, priorities, and planning, you are leaving the future to chance."

This, most often, stems from overconfidence, perfectionism, and insecurity. It is further reinforced by our need to chase after achievements. Fortunately, fixing this issue is baked into correctly managing time. We'll go over prioritization and goal setting in Chapter 2 and effective communication further along. These skills will serve us well in not falling victim to this.

Additionally, many colleagues have struggled with saying 'no.' It is counterintuitive to say that to do better at work, you should decline certain tasks. Yet, if one simply accepts all tasks they are qualified for, it's easier for them to become overworked. Not only that, but it also snowballs into that special quality, turning from valuable to common and replaceable. I'm not recommending you lead a revolt against your boss because they tried to ask too much. Instead, approach the problem diplomatically. Remind them of your current workload, and address how the new task could negatively impact the company. Oddly, you can find a solution where the entire team works efficiently.

While these two pitfalls are very common, there are plenty more that we have yet to mention. Some of them, like miscommunication and procrastination, are addressed later in the book. Let's not get ahead of ourselves, though. I invite you to reflect, if for a few minutes, on the struggles you've faced while managing time. Write it down and give some ideas as to how you'd combat it.

You found another area of the book where you'll want to read particularly closely. Or this sore spot is very specific. In any case, applying the structures in this book should help significantly. It may just leave a tiny wrinkle. And that's ok. Wrinkles can be ironed out.

Next, think about some of your fortés in Time Management. Are you great at making easy-to-follow charts? Or are you excellent at analyzing data? Your speciality is cleanly sectioning off parts of a project! Any of these, and many more skills, will serve you. Don't be scared to be creative when thinking of these. My college roommate was a great cook, allowing him to start every morning just right. You'll want to make note of these strengths, just like you did with your struggles.

Poor time management often affects us negatively. Most obviously, it can harshly impact our work performance. It's been shown that failing to manage time and projects correctly often leads to partial or full losses, making time for new ventures more difficult. And while that much is evident and harmful to us, the opposite is true. Let's look at some more benefits you may reap from optimizing how you spend each hour.

Achieving Attention To Delay

Plan of action: Use these strategies to stop procrastinating and boost your productivity.

Procrastination is the silent productivity killer that impacts people in all spheres of life. Everyone has been guilty of procrastinating important tasks and seeing precious time slip away. So don't be alarmed! We cover a lot of ground in the pamphlet "Procrastination No More," including how to overcome procrastination and unlock your potential. Together, we'll implement a comprehensive strategy to eliminate procrastination and increase your output.

How to Resolve the Mysteries of Procrastination

Examine the psychology of putting things off.

Acknowledge the different types of procrastinators and the things that usually trigger them.

The Cost of Procrastination

Consider the unintended consequences of chronic procrastination.

Understand the impact on your goals, well-being, and overall standard of living.

How to Break the Procrastination Cycle

Identify the routines that promote procrastination.

Learn how to interrupt these patterns and establish new, productive ones.

Knowing Oneself Is Power

Become acutely aware of the ways in which you procrastinate.

Apply self-awareness to implement customised transformation strategies.

Methods for Completing Tasks

Discover how to beat procrastination with a collection of tried-and-true techniques.

Inspiration and Objective Establishment

Decide on clear, motivating goals that will motivate you to act.

Reward yourself and visualise your goals to stay on course.

Acknowledge the relationship between perfectionism and procrastination.

Recognise your flaws and accept that growth is more important than perfection.

the Distraction Dragon is in check

Acknowledge the origins of your daily distractions.

Employ strategies to lessen or eliminate these distractions.

Effective Time Management

Gain proficiency in time management to prevent procrastinating.

Gain knowledge of time management techniques to increase output.

Setting Priorities

It's critical to prioritise and select the most critical and urgent tasks and activities in addition to setting clear objectives.

By doing this, you may prevent procrastination and focus your attention on the most important activities.

Value Analysis: Assess each task's significance and worth in light of your aims and objectives.

Does this task make a major contribution to reaching my goals? If not, think about removing or assigning it to save time for more pertinent tasks.

Results should be the main priority, along with long-term effects.

Sort the tasks according to importance based on how they will affect your objectives and desired results.

Establishing and Evaluating Priorities

Prioritisation management is a continuous activity.

You must constantly evaluate and revise your priorities as new demands and situations emerge.

The following advice will help you efficiently manage your priorities:

Periodic Review: Make time to go over your priorities on a frequent basis.

Depending on your circumstances and the demands of the moment, this could be done on a daily, weekly, or monthly basis.

Flexibility: Allow yourself to change your priorities when necessary.

Unexpected events or fresh information can occasionally necessitate reevaluating and rearranging your workload.

Communication and Negotiation: It's critical to discuss your priorities and work out deadlines and expectations with all parties involved while working in a team or having shared duties.

By doing this, unneeded conflict is avoided, and everyone's priorities are in line.

Recognising the Effects of Ineffective Time Management

Ineffective time management can have a big impact on a lot of different areas of our lives. Here are a few instances:

1. Stress and anxiety: Inadequate time management can lead to stress and worry as we struggle to fulfil obligations, meet deadlines, and accomplish our goals.

Consider the following scenario: you have a project that is due in a week, so you put it off for a few days and then try to finish it all in one day. Stress, anxiety, and overwhelm can have an adverse effect on your general well-being and performance.

2. Opportunities lost: Ineffective time management can also result in opportunities lost. Ineffective time management can cause us to lose out on chances for social interaction,

professional development, and personal development. For instance, you risk missing the deadline and losing the chance if you put off applying for a scholarship or a job.

3. Low productivity and performance: Ineffective management might influence our output and productivity. We could find it difficult to meet deadlines, finish projects quickly, and accomplish our objectives. This may affect how well we succeed at work or school and how well we reach our objectives.

For instance, you can score poorly on an exam and find it difficult to get the grade you want if you spend hours on social media or watching TV instead of preparing.

4. Relationship tension: Ineffective time management can also affect how we interact with others. Prioritising unproductive pursuits over spending time with loved ones or taking care of our obligations can strain our

relationships and negatively affect our general well-being.

For example, poor time management might cause arguments and hurt feelings if you routinely forget to make time for your family or relationship.

5. Finally, ineffective time management might result in burnout. We risk burnout and exhaustion if we don't prioritise self-care and time management on a regular basis.

For instance, if you often put in lengthy workdays without taking breaks or caring for yourself, you run the risk of burning out and experiencing both physical and mental tiredness.

In summary, ineffective time management can have a big impact on a lot of different areas of our lives. Knowing the negative effects of ineffective time management can help us prioritise time management strategies, accomplish our objectives, and improve our general well-being. These repercussions can include stress and worry, missed opportunities, low performance and productivity, strained relationships, and burnout.

Setting Priorities for Your Objectives

Setting priorities for your objectives is essential to efficient time management. It entails determining which objectives are most essential to you and allocating your time and energy to completing those tasks first. To assist you in prioritising your goals, consider the following steps:

1. Create a list of all your objectives: Begin by listing all the objectives you hope to accomplish. These could be long-term or short-term, professional or personal, or any other objectives that are significant to you.

2. Next, assess each aim according to its significance, immediacy, and applicability. Consider asking yourself the following questions:

- How significant is this objective to me?
- Can this aim be accomplished at any time, or is there a deadline?
- In what way does this objective fit into my larger vision and mission?

3. Sort your objectives: Divide your objectives into three groups: high, medium, and low priority. Goals classified as high-priority are the most crucial and urgent, medium-priority are significant but less urgent, and low-priority are less critical and may wait till later.

4. Prioritise your goals: Give your time and energy to accomplish your top priorities first. This will guarantee that you are attending to the most pressing needs first and assist you in moving closer to your most critical goals.

5. While it's crucial to concentrate on high-priority objectives, you should also allocate a fair amount of time and resources to medium- and low-priority goals. This will enable you to

prioritise your most crucial goals while still moving closer to these goals.

6. Review and modify your priorities on a regular basis: Review and modify your priorities on a frequent basis in light of changes in your life, objectives, and situation. This will assist you in staying on course and guarantee that you are moving closer to your most crucial goals.

For instance, suppose your objectives are as follows:

- Introduce a new, highly-important product.
- Boost customer support (moderate priority)
- Acquire a low-priority new skill.

Due to its high priority and immediacy, you would direct your time and resources towards the launch of a new product first. Then, since acquiring a new skill and enhancing customer service are both medium- and low-priority objectives, you would divide your time and resources between them.

In summary, setting priorities for your objectives is an essential part of efficient time management. You can move closer to your most significant Creatives and chapter success by creating a list of all your objectives, assessing each one, classifying your goals, concentrating on high-priority goals, striking a balance between medium- and low-priority goals, and routinely analysing and revising your priorities.

Selecting the Correct Chair

One of the most important choices you make for your workstation is the chair you use. Using any comfortable chair from home as a desk chair is simple and convenient. Your productivity will suffer as your back starts to pain. You cannot concentrate on your task if you are in agony. For this reason, you should spend money on a supportive and comfortable office chair.

An excellent office chair should have wheels, be adjustable, and support your lower back. You may change the chair's height, as well as the armrests and seat, thanks to these capabilities. You won't have to scrape the floor when slipping in and out of your workstation thanks to the wheels. Instead of merely ordering a chair and crossing your fingers, it is best to test it out first. This can help you determine the proper chair characteristics based on your weight and height.

Appropriate Lighting

Lighting in a home office is frequently overlooked. All of us make the error of presuming that the room's lighting is adequate. Insufficient lighting often prompts most individuals to go acquire a desk lamp. These two choices are incorrect. First of all, the room's lighting should not only be adequate to illuminate your desk but it should also be positioned so as to minimise needless glare. The light source ought to be above you, not in your line of sight or reflecting off your screen.

Desk lamps are not a good choice because of this. Their direct light might cause eye strain and create a glare on your screen.

The same holds for daylight that streams in via windows. It's wonderful to have natural lighting. However, unless trees or curtains shade it, it should never be directly behind you or to the side. Otherwise, it will be difficult to view your screen when the sun comes through. For extended periods, it's also critical to adjust the screen's brightness to protect your eyes. However, as eye sensitivity varies, this will not work for everyone.

Online Resources

Working from home is much simpler, thanks to the internet. Having said that, if it is an issue, it can also be annoying. If you want to work from home, you'll need a fast and dependable internet connection. This is particularly valid if you frequently attend calls or meetings. Suppose you have to ask individuals to repeat themselves during a meeting because your internet is slowing down, or you run the risk of missing important information. In that case, it can come out as unprofessional. As a result, you should confirm that your internet service provider is reputable and capable of offering 50 Mbps or more of internet speed.

Additional Devices and Attachments

When setting up your home office, the things on the above list are the most crucial. On the other hand, you can purchase additional accessories to facilitate your work-from-home lifestyle. For calls and meetings, for instance, having a headset is essential. These days, you may also acquire ones that filter out background sounds from your environment. As a result, while you speak, others won't be able to hear your neighbour's dogs barking.

If you buy a larger screen, it's also a good idea to have a keyboard, mouse, or touchpad. It's simpler to use these external devices than your laptop's keyboard and touchpad. Of course, if you are using a desktop computer, this won't be required. Also, having a multipurpose printer can be useful, even though we operate mostly in digital format. There are instances when printing or scanning documents is unavoidable.

An uninterruptible power supply (UPS) or surge protector is a great investment for people who work from home. In the event of a power outage, this shields your computer from surges. Additionally, you can get a tiny UPS for your modem, which will maintain internet access during a blackout. The amount of time your laptop battery will survive before needing to be charged, though, limits this. Even so, it's a terrific alternative because it lets you keep your job and let others know that you won't be available right away rather than being disconnected right away.

You can also have speakers if you enjoy listening to music while working. This will enhance audio quality and eliminate the need for constant headphone use. For a workspace, a smart assistant is also not a bad idea. Not only will it store your thoughts for later, but it will also aid in your memory of crucial calls and meetings. When I'm working, I frequently get an idea or thought and ask my smart assistant to record it for later. If hiring an office assistant is out of the question, a whiteboard can work just as well. It will help you work on things visually or quickly scribble down items to remember later. If you utilise it to organise your day, it can also assist you in being more productive.

A yoga mat is an additional fantastic item to have on a desk. Working from home makes it simple to become engrossed for hours at a time and forget to take little breaks. This is the reason that treadmills and standing desks have been so well-liked lately. However, having a yoga mat close by will serve as a helpful reminder to take a few minutes to pause and exercise your body. Your body will appreciate the impact that even a few easy stretches can make. Having plants on your desk is also a terrific way to improve your mood. Having plants around will also motivate you to check on their growth or water them sometimes.

Make a menu for the next week.

For single mothers, creating a weekly food plan and following it by purchasing the necessary goods are crucial. Their lives are made easier and more organised by this practice, which has several benefits.

First of all, it facilitates effective budgeting since single mothers may arrange their meals around reasonably priced and healthful selections, cutting down on wasteful spending. They also avoid having to think about what to cook every day, which saves them significant time during busy workdays.

Furthermore, since meal plans enable single mothers to prepare a range of nutrient-dense meals for their families, they encourage healthier eating practices.

Additionally, when foods are bought with a specific purpose in mind, it reduces food waste.

A weekly meal plan makes it easier for single mothers to shop for groceries, encourages frugal spending and guarantees that, despite their hectic schedules, they can still feed their families healthful, pleasant meals.

Keep snacks in pantry baskets that are easily accessible.

For single mothers, keeping snacks in easily accessible pantry baskets is a useful tip that can greatly streamline everyday tasks.

Snacks should be organised and easily accessible because single mothers frequently have little time and may need to multitask during the day.

Snacking in a messy pantry may be chaotic and stressful. By organising snacks into baskets, you can create a dedicated space where you and your kids can find what you need fast.

Your kids will also benefit from this arrangement since it makes it simple for them to get a snack when they get hungry.

Single mothers can also take inventory more efficiently by arranging snacks in baskets, which makes meal preparation and purchase lists simpler.

It's a simple but effective step that will help you keep your home tidy, make snack time hassle-free, and free up valuable time for other essential chores and meaningful time with your kids.

To assist with food portioning for the week, use a slow cooker.

This kitchen tool has many benefits in addition to making meal preparation easier. Single mothers frequently balance a lot of duties, which leaves little time for cooking. They can prepare wholesome, home-cooked meals using a slow cooker without needing continual supervision.

They save a tonne of time and energy over the week by cooking in bulk because one slow cooker session can prepare several meals. By dividing the food into portions, she can give her kids easy grab-and-go options and relieve herself of the burden of preparing and arranging meals every day.

Moreover, buying items in bulk might result in cost savings when utilising a slow cooker. Because mothers may incorporate an abundance of veggies and lean proteins into their dishes, it also promotes healthier eating habits.

Essentially, a slow cooker turns into a dependable kitchen buddy, guaranteeing that single mothers can serve their families healthful, home-cooked meals while keeping a reasonable and less demanding daily schedule.

Prepared meals can be kept in the freezer or refrigerator by using a vacuum sealer.

Meal made and stored in the refrigerator or freezer with a vacuum sealer is a clever and useful tip that especially helps single mothers. For someone who frequently balances a busy schedule with multiple obligations, preparing meals ahead of time can be really helpful.

Food is kept fresher longer by the vacuum sealer's capacity to eliminate air from storage bags, which keeps food from going bad or getting freezer burn.

This cuts grocery costs and food waste in addition to saving time. In their spare time, single mothers can cook larger quantities of food and split them out into individual servings for convenient consumption later.

This strategy reduces the burden involved in everyday cooking while also guaranteeing their kids have access to wholesome and delectable meals.

It's an efficient and convenient investment that frees up single mothers to concentrate on other important facets of their lives, knowing that nutritious selections are readily available and mealtime is made simple.

The Eisenhower Matrix

In Daily Life, Juggling A Variety Of Obligations And Chores Can Be Very Difficult. The Eisenhower Matrix Is Among The Best Instruments To Tackle This Problem. Eisenhower Was Renowned For His Adept Handling Of Duties And Obligations.

A Visual Tool Called The Eisenhower Matrix Is Used To Classify Jobs According To Their Relevance And Urgency. There Are Four Quadrants In The Matrix:

Quadrant I: Urgent And Important Jobs Are Those That Require Your Immediate Attention. These Could Be Urgent Issues, Catastrophes, Or Tasks With Approaching Due Dates. Your Highest Priorities Should Be The Tasks In This Area.

Important But Not Urgent (Quadrant Ii): These Are The Non-Urgent Chores That Support Your Long-Term Objectives And Core Beliefs. These Could Involve Relationship-Building, Strategic Planning, Or Personal Growth. It Would Help If You Made Time For These Chores Since They Can Help You Achieve Your Long-Term Objectives And Avert Catastrophes.

Quadrant Iii: Urgent But Not Important: This Quadrant Includes Chores That Need Your Urgent Attention But Don't Really Advance Your Values Or Goals. Interruptions Or Certain Daily Duties May Be The Cause. As Much As You Can, You Should Attempt To Assign These Chores To Others.

Not Urgent And Not Important (Quadrant Iv): These Are The Non-Value-Adding Activities That Can Divert Your Attention From Your Objectives. These Chores Frequently Serve As Time Wasters Or Distractions. As Many Of

These Things As You Can Should Be Crossed Off Your To-Do List.

The Simplicity Of The Eisenhower Matrix Is What Makes It So Beautiful. It Makes It Simple For You To See How Important And Urgent Each Of Your Jobs Is, Which Can Help You Set Priorities And Make The Most Use Of Your Time.

When You Use This Matrix Effectively, You May Focus More On The Chores That Really Move You Closer To Your Goals And Experience A Decrease In Stress And Increase In Productivity. But It's Critical To Keep In Mind That The Matrix Is Not A Panacea. To Make It Function Correctly, It Must Be Paired With Constancy, Discipline, And Willpower.

To Put It Briefly, The Eisenhower Matrix Is A Tool That Assists You In Differentiating Between Urgent And Significant Tasks. We'll Look At How To Apply This Matrix To Your Everyday Tasks And How It Can Help You

Manage Your Time Better In The Parts That Follow.

Self-Soothing For General Health

Taking Care Of One's Own Physical, Mental, And Emotional Health Is Known As Self-Care. It Entails Accepting Accountability For One's Hwell-Being Wellbeing And Implementing The Required Adjustments To Enhance It. Taking Care Of Oneself Involves Not Just One's Physical Health But Also One's Mental And Emotional Wellness.

There Are Various Categories Under Which Self-Care Can Be Classified, Such As Mental, Emotional, And Physical Self-Care. Exercise, A Healthy Diet, Getting Adequate Sleep, And Abstaining From Drugs Are All Examples Of Physical Self-Care. Writing, Reading, Practising Mindfulness, And Meditation Are Examples Of Mental Self-Care. Journaling, Counselling, And Engaging In Self-Compassion Exercises Are Examples Of Emotional Self-Care.

It's Critical To Practise Physical Self-Care To Preservwell-Being Wellbeing. Maintaining Physical Health Also Requires Eating A Balanced Diet Since It Gives The Body The Nutrition It Needs To Function Correctly. Physical Health Also Benefits From Getting Enough Sleep Since It Enables The Body To Mend And Regenerate. Maintaining Abstinence From Dangerous Substances Like Smoking And Excessive Alcohol Intake Can Also Enhance Well-Being Well-Being.

Maintaining Mental Health And Lowering The Risk Of Mental Health Problems Like Depression And Anxiety Need Mental Self-Care. Because Reading And Writing Can Enhance Cognitive Function And Lower Stress Levels, They Can Be Utilised As A Kind Of Mental Self-Care. Since They Can Lessen Anxiety And Increase Focus, Mindfulness Exercises And Meditation Can Also Be Utilised As A Kind Of Mental Self-Care.

Maintaining Well-Being Wellbeing And Lowering The Risk Of Emotional Illnesses Like Depression And Anxiety Require Emotional Self-Care. Since Journaling Enables People To Process Their Feelings And Ideas, It Can Be Utilised As An Emotional Self-Care Tool. As It Enables People To Talk To A Professional About Their Feelings And Ideas, Seeing A Therapist Can Also Be Utilised As A Kind Of Emotional Self-Care. Being Kind And Understanding To Oneself Is Made Possible By Engaging In Self-Compassion Practices, Which Can Also Be Utilised As An Emotional Self-Care Strategy.

Being Aware Of One's Own Physical, Mental, And Well-Being Wellbeing Is A Continuous Practice That Goes Into Self-Care. It's Critical To Incorporate Self-Care Into Everyday Activities And To Remember To Take Care Of Oneself Even Throughout Trying Circumstances. It's Also Critical To Keep In Mind That Self-Care

Entails A Lifetime Commitment To Looking After Oneself Rather Than A Quick Fix.

Apart From The Pursuits Above, Self-Care Might Encompass Activities Such As Taking Walks In The Outdoors, Enjoying Music, Engaging In Yoga, Or Creating A Skincare Regimen. It's Also Critical To Have A Strong Social Network. Developing And Upholding Positive Relationships With Friends And Family Can Be A Crucial Part Of Self-Care Since They Give People A Feeling Of Community And Emotional Support.

Self-Care Can Improve One's Physical, Mental, And Well-Being Wellbeing And Is Crucial For Well-Being Well-Being. It's Critical To Incorporate Self-Care Into Everyday Activities And To Remember To Take Care Of Oneself Even Throughout Trying Circumstances. Always Remember To Treat Yourself With Compassion And Kindness And Commit To Self-Care For The Rest Of Your Life.

Ava Was A Young Woman Who Lived In A Tiny Village Tucked Away In The Middle Of A Forest Once. Nothing Pleased Ava More Than To Assist Others; She Was A Kind And Compassionate Person. All Those Who Knew Her Loved And Respected Her, And She Devoted Her Days To Serving The Needs Of Her Community.

Ava Managed A Busy Schedule, Yet She Always Found Time For Herself. She Made Sure To Practise Self-Care In A Number Of Ways Every Day Since She Felt That It Was Crucial To Preserve Well-Being. She Would Take A Gentle Yoga Class In The Morning, Eat A Hearty Meal, And Then Go Outside And Enjoy The Beauty Of The Surrounding Forest.

Ava Scheduled Time For Mental Wellness As Well. She Loved To Read And Kept A Journal, And She Discovered That These Activities Allowed Her To Decompress And Work Through Her Feelings. She Also Discovered That Mindfulness And Meditation Training

Enabled Her To Manage Her Stress And Remain In The Present.

For Ava, Emotional Self-Care Was Essential. She Understood That In Order For Her To Be Able To Assist Others, She Needed To Take Care Of Her Emotional Health. She Made Sure To Schedule Time Every Day To Communicate With Her Family And Let Them Know How She Felt. She Also Discovered That Being Gentle And Understanding With Oneself Was Facilitated By Her Self-Compassion Practices.

Ava's Self-Care Regimen Developed To Become A Regular Element Of Her Daily Schedule Over Time. She Discovered That By Looking For Herself, She Could Better Look After Other People. She Became Well-Known As A Ray Of Hope And Light In The Village, And Her Neighbours Looked To Her For Leadership And Encouragement.

One Day, A Powerful Storm Tore Through The Community, Destroying And Wreaking

Extensive Damage. Without Delay, Ava Became Involved In Assisting Her Fellow Peasants In Reconstructing Their Houses And Livelihoods. She Put In Endless Effort, Day And Night, To Aid In The Recovery Of Her Neighbourhood.

Ava Never Lost Sight Of The Significance Of Self-Care, Even In The Face Of The Daunting Task At Her. She Was Careful To Take Pauses And Practise Self-Care Whenever She Could. She Understood That She Would Be In A Better Position To Care For Others If She Took Care Of Herself.

The Town Was Able To Recover And Rebuild Because Of Ava's Unrelenting Devotion To Self-Care. The People In Ava's Community Knew They Could Always Rely On Her For Support And Direction, And They Would Always Be Thankful To Her.

Everyone Who Knew Ava Saw Her As An Inspiration For Self-Care After That Day.

The Conclusion.

It's Crucial To Understand That The Narrative Is Made Up And Not Based On Any Actual Person Or Circumstance. The Narrative Merely Served To Illustrate How Self-Care May Be Incorporated Into Daily Life And How It Can Be For The Well-Being And Wellbeing Of People Around Them.

Although It's Not Always Simple, Discipline Is Necessary To Take Control Of Our Bodies. We May Get The Desired Level Of Physical Mastery By Establishing A Specific Objective, Creating A Strategy, And Persistently Working Towards It. Through Discipline, Perseverance, And Overcoming Obstacles, We Can Change Our Physical Appearance And Enhance Our General Health. We Can Actually Control Our Bodies And Reach Our Full Potential Via Discipline.

Breaking Down Procrastination

Procrastination – the universal enemy of productivity and progress. We've all experienced those moments when we put off important tasks in favour of less pressing matters. Have you ever found yourself postponing tasks, watching the hours slip away, only to feel a pang of regret later? If so, you've experienced the grip of procrastination, a formidable force that can impede progress and hinder personal growth. In this chapter, we're diving headfirst into the intricate web of procrastination, unravelling its causes, understanding its effects, and equipping you with strategies to conquer this common challenge.

It's a seemingly harmless action, one we've all indulged in at some point. However, its impact reaches beyond mere delay – it can create a ripple effect* that touches various aspects of our lives. From uncompleted projects to missed opportunities, procrastination has the power to stifle progress. * The ripple effect - demonstrates how our actions create a series of outcomes that extend beyond their initial impact. Understanding this concept prompts us to make mindful choices, considering the broader consequences they might have on our future well-being and success.

In the upcoming scenarios, I'll take you through a series of short stories that vividly illustrate the procrastination effect, from its initial seeds to its full-grown impact, helping you grasp its significance and implications in real-life situations.

Imagine Sarah, a diligent student with big dreams of becoming a successful writer. She has a term paper due in a month, but she constantly puts off starting it. She thinks, "I have plenty of time, and I work better under pressure." So, she spends her days watching TV, going out with friends, and avoiding her assignments.

As the due date approaches, Sarah realizes she's in trouble. She starts researching and writing frantically, sacrificing sleep and stressing herself out. The final paper is rushed lacking depth and creativity. She gets a passing grade, but her professor notes missed opportunities for excellence.

In this scenario, Sarah's initial decision to procrastinate had a ripple effect. It affected her overall grade, her stress levels, and the quality of her work. If she had started early and worked consistently, she could have produced an outstanding paper that showcased her true abilities. This example highlights how seemingly small choices can set off a chain reaction of outcomes that impact various areas of our lives. Understanding the ripple effect can inspire us to make proactive choices that lead to better results and fulfilment in the long run.

He envisions creating a platform that connects local artisans with a global audience, showcasing their unique handmade creations.

At first, Lucas is fueled by excitement and enthusiasm. He spends hours sketching out his business plan, envisioning the website layout, and brainstorming marketing strategies. However, as the days turn into weeks, Lucas finds himself caught in the web of procrastination.

Instead of taking immediate action and diving into the tasks that will propel his venture forward, Lucas starts to delay. He convinces himself that he needs more time to perfect his plan, fine-tune his strategies, and gather more resources.

Weeks turn into months, and Lucas's grand vision remains confined to the pages of his notebook. He watches as days slip by, all the while underestimating the power of procrastination. His motivation wanes, and doubt begins to creep in.

Lucas's hesitation not only affects his business dream but also starts to take a toll on his confidence and self-esteem. As he watches other entrepreneurs launch their ventures and witness their progress, he can't help but feel left behind. The ripple effect of his procrastination becomes evident. Opportunities that could have been seized slip away, potential partners move on to other collaborations, and the initial excitement fades into frustration.

The scenario of Lucas vividly highlights how procrastination, when left unchecked, can erode the foundations of even the most promising dreams. As we delve deeper into understanding the procrastination effect, you'll find strategies and insights to help you avoid similar pitfalls and keep your aspirations on track.

Let's meet Ana, a nature enthusiast who has always dreamed of owning her own florist business. She envisions a charming boutique filled with vibrant blooms, a place where customers can find the perfect bouquet for any occasion.

Ana's passion for flowers is undeniable. She spends her free time studying various flower species, attending workshops, and experimenting with floral arrangements. She even has a notebook filled with sketches and ideas for her future shop's interior design.

Excitement bubbles within Ana as she imagines herself arranging stunning bouquets and helping customers find the ideal flowers for their special moments. However, as the months go by, Ana's dream remains a concept on paper. She hesitates to take the first step, fearing that her skills might not be good enough or that the market might be too competitive. She tells herself that she needs more training, more experience, and more time to save money before she can launch her business.

The procrastination effect starts to set in. Ana's dream, once full of vibrancy and enthusiasm, begins to lose its lustre. She finds herself scrolling through social media, looking at other florists' success stories, while her dream gathers dust.

As Ana delayed her plans, her confidence took a hit. She starts doubting her abilities and questioning whether her dream is worth pursuing. The longer she waits, the harder it becomes to take that crucial first step.

The ripple effect of Ana's procrastination becomes evident in missed opportunities. She could have started small, perhaps by selling her arrangements at local markets or hosting floral workshops. Instead, she watches as others seize similar chances and build their floral empires.

The story of Ana illustrates how procrastination can smother even the most passionate dreams. In our exploration of the procrastination effect, you'll uncover ways to break free from its grip and transform your aspirations into reality. By identifying procrastination patterns, adopting effective strategies, and embracing a proactive mindset, you'll empower yourself to overcome the challenges and uncertainties that hold you back.

By recognizing these patterns, embracing effective strategies, and fostering a proactive mindset, you'll empower yourself to break free from the cycle of procrastination. The goal is to transform your aspirations from mere dreams into tangible accomplishments, bridging the gap between where you are now and where you want to be. So, let's continue our exploration of the procrastination effect and arm ourselves with the tools needed to overcome its challenges and achieve our goals.

www.ingramcontent.com/pod-product-compliance
Lightning Source LLC
Chambersburg PA
CBHW052149110526
44591CB00012B/1905